AROUND THE WORLD
IN NINETY YEARS

CLOUGH WILLIAMS-ELLIS

AROUND THE WORLD
IN NINETY YEARS

GOLDEN DRAGON BOOKS
PORTMEIRION · PENRHYNDEUDRAETH · GWYNEDD
1978

First published 1978
Published by Portmeirion Limited
Printed in Great Britain by
Robert MacLehose and Company Limited
Printers to the University of Glasgow

LIMP :— ISBN 0.216.90694.6

CASED :— ISBN 0216.90695.4

To

PEGGY POLLARD. My most gallant Comrade-in-Arms
in uncounted Conservation battles, for her
generous help in the shaping of this book,

and to

CHARLOTTE DORRIEN SMITH. For so ingeniously
editing my disparate bits and pieces into the
semblance of an actual book,

and to
my son-in-law

EUAN COOPER-WILLIS. For constructive advice generally,

and also to

ROBERT SAKULA. As my Longstop.

The Author gratefully acknowledges his indebtedness to *The Guardian*, *The Times*, *The Listener*, *House and Garden*, *The Western Mail*, *The Spectator*, *Punch*, and any other periodicals or journals for such material as he has resurrected or quoted from their columns.

The engraving at the head of each chapter is reproduced from *The Universal Penman*, published by George Bickham between 1733 and 1743.

Contents

	LIST OF PLATES	ix
	FOREWORD—A DECLARATION	xi
1	YET ANOTHER BOOK? WHY?	1
2	THE NEW DEAL. FALTERING STEPS	5
3	THE BRITISH METEOR—1951	13
4	GREAT EXPECTATIONS	18
5	A CRISS-CROSS RECONNAISSANCE	26
6	THAT SIXTH SENSE—DREAMS	39
7	MEN, WOMEN AND BUILDINGS	45
8	A PEEK AT AMERICA	57
9	FOOD, LOVELY FOOD	61
10	VAINGLORY	68
11	AROUND THE MEDITERRANEAN	77
12	THE MIRACLE OF PORT GRIMAUD	88
13	PORTMEIRION GROWS UP	95
14	DIVERSIONS AND DIAMONDS	101
15	THE AUTHOR'S CREDO—MY POSITIVELY FINAL APPEARANCE	112
16	AS OF NOW	118
	EPILOGUE—HERE ENDETH	125
	INDEX	129

List of Plates

Plate 1   Temple in fibreglass at Hatton Grange, Shropshire, later repeated elsewhere *facing page* 36

Plate 2a   The author's first country house, Llangoed Castle, Breconshire, 1912 . . .   37

Plate 2b   . . . And his last, Dalton Hall, Cumbria, 1973   37

Plate 3a   The author, at the age of ninety, inspecting the roof timbers at Dalton Hall   52

Plate 3b   Nantclwyd Hall, the new south front   52

Plate 4a   Nantclwyd Hall, bridge carrying the new drive   53

Plate 4b   The re-modelled village street at Cornwell, Oxfordshire   53

Plate 5a   The *Oronsay* (foreground) moored in the harbour at Portofino   84

Plate 5b   Port Grimaud   84

Plate 6a   Rhiwlas, near Bala, a new manor house in the local vernacular   85

Plate 6b   The Cliff House, the latest addition at Portmeirion   85

Plate 7   A cartoon by Hans Feibusch R.A. in the Dome at Portmeirion   100

Plate 8   The author and Lady Williams-Ellis at the Portmeirion Golden Jubilee Carnival in 1976   101

Foreword

A Declaration

In the almost perfect state, every person shall have at least ten years of easy,
carefree, happy living before he dies.

Thus Don Marquis in his *The Almost Perfect State*, a book I have
long treasured for the reckless gaiety of his humane philosophy,
which I find most endearing.

So what?

Well, at handsomely over ninety, I have, in all probability,
already *had* the last ten years of my life, and they have certainly
been 'easy, carefree and happy' to a miracle; a mere continuation
indeed of a quite singularly fortunate existence, from the early
eighties of the last century to the mid-seventies of this.

My surprising 90th birthday, some years ago now, was greeted
by kind friends with 'Bravo! Now for your 100th'. But why? I am
entirely content with my still reasonable score, as how should I
not be, in that, over all, fate has been so kind?

Inevitably, one's faculties must decline, and old age, soon or
late, brings them to a nadir, when their inadequacy must
infuriate oneself and become burdensome to one's friends. With

a merciful exit at hand, let no-one dare obstruct it. For I regard dying as no more than a most interesting once-for-all experience, the 'Finis' at the end of one's book of life.

Inevitably, one leaves something behind one—good or ill—that, if only microscopically, remains embedded in humanity's total experience, if no more significantly than one grain of sand in the whole Sahara.

Amid humanity's general hubbub, one small squeak has been mine, pleading the cause of beauty.

I may have done little good, but I am not conscious of having done much harm, and I shall enter oblivion with complete composure, my last words, if any:

Cherish the Past, Adorn the Present and Construct for the Future.

I

Yet Another Book? Why?

The very title of this latest and probably last book of mine will have suggested that I am a pretty qualified member of that large and ever-growing order of what are now politely called 'Senior Citizens', to whom various concessions have been generously made as some compensation for their assumed disabilities and diminished earning power. Aware of my own senior status, half-way between 90 and 100, in this now enormous army and aware too that I was nonetheless still in pretty good working order, a thoughtful and benevolent friend suddenly startled me thus: 'As somehow or other you yourself seem to have reached a sort of "Plateau of Serenity" in your extreme old age, where you still find life interesting, enjoyable and thoroughly worthwhile, why not enlarge on that and how you reached it. That should be of direct interest and perhaps help, to the many in our ageing population who are contemplating their own old age with doubts and misgivings, if not with actual dismay.' This prod coupled with continuing and apparently insatiable appetite for more information displayed by my friends, my family and many complete strangers as to my life, my works and my opinions, have encouraged me to have another stab at autobiography.

My first instalment, published in 1928 as *The Architect* ran through several editions. It was superseded in 1971 by an updated version, *Architect Errant*. However, unexpectedly, my life has gone on and on. Moreover it has been pointed out to me that in that book I dismissed the 32-year period from 1945 in a mere thirty pages and that this last (or latest) third of my life deserved fuller treatment. So here goes. I hope that those who need it may glean some little indirect help from it, while the idly curious gain answers to their questions. If the former should feel, when half way through the book, that they are being cheated of such guidance, then they can swiftly turn to the last chapter, where I have set out such 'Signposts' as I myself have found of use, both in the attainment and in the maintenance of a contented 'nonagenarianage'.

The Second German War brought with it an almost immediate and total ban against all private building; the calling up of all able-bodied workers; the holding back of all materials from private use and the actual requisition of any stocks deemed to be of even remote use to the government. All this bore not only on my profession of architect but upon my now flourishing but still only half grown 'offspring', Portmeirion, as well. Here even the most obviously necessary maintenance works were closely monitored and all supplies to the hotel strictly rationed. Moreover, we were clearly heading for a much changed world where the wages of staff might come to equal, or even surpass, the incomes of some of our former clientele. The new regulations and reforms imposed by Ernest Bevin, in his generally well-justified Catering and Wages Act, inevitably added to the place's running costs. I had discussed his proposals with Bevan himself, and was fully persuaded of their justice but nonetheless the actual survival of the whole Portmeirion set-up seemed in jeopardy. How actually the transition was handled, is told in a later chapter.

Because of the necessary channelling of architects and building materials into the process of rebuilding, and the provision of services and amenities throughout the country, the 'private patron' almost disappeared. Indeed, as I myself discovered, he

was even forbidden to indulge in the most public-spirited enterprise. The State as patron emerged triumphant, with unrivalled
chances in our bombed and battered cities, particularly London,
both for a rational new deal in lay-out and for magnanimity in the
individual buildings.

That the young architect who only practised for the first time
in the years after the war had no very gay time is, alas, most
sadly true. The usual routine bread and butter war damage jobs,
dilapidations and state housing schemes in which he spent
laborious days as a salaried assistant in some public authority's
office, were scarcely intoxicating. Yet even an urban re-housing
project carried out with the economy that the shortages imposed,
and strictly conditioned by practical, economic, industrial and
social requirements, immediately reveal if its designers have eyes
or not. There will be a hundred unmistakeable signs that all needs
have been duly provided for, not only with efficiency but with
grace, which too is surely a need in any society claiming to be
civilized.

For a period, British architecture and British architects went
into almost total eclipse. Inevitably. But eclipse, whether total or
partial, does not connote any diminution in the intensity of the
source of light. Merely that some obstructive body has temporarily
supervened to cast its shadow. The War and its aftermath, in
short, blacked out architecture even more thoroughly than the
other arts of peace, and put it almost completely to bed for at
least a decade.

Yet it is in bed, so we used to be told, that one did one's
growing, and whether that is true or not of little boys, it did
seem to be true of architecture, which in the late 1940s showed
signs of having piled up a tremendous head of new energy that
should have poured brilliantly forth immediately genuine peace
reopened the sluices. For a time this was actually so, in many of
our blitzed cities, not only in the special set-pieces of architectural fireworks officially promoted as the Festival of Britain, but
in hopeful little patches of gay and intelligent designing scattered
here and there throughout Britain.

Tragically the impetus was not maintained—the excitement
and delight of the Festival, even of Lansbury and the first of the

New Towns, soon fell victim to the economic pressures of the State. The government's demand for maximum returns, or at least the appearance of them, for money spent, led to the advocates of 'free' architecture and brutalism being given full reign. Far too many of our helpless citizens were re-housed in tower blocks that were as extravagant to build as they were hateful to inhabit. In the City of London itself, private developers followed the philistine fashions set by public example; new office blocks, pushful reflections of New York's legitimate skyscrapers engulfed the fifty or so spires that had given London its own unique skyline, and even threatened the great bubble dome of St. Paul's itself, the work of our greatest architect, and the admiration and delight of the world for centuries.

2

The New Deal. Faltering Steps

As I have just outlined, the war and taxation had greatly reduced, or even I feared permanently killed off, the species, wealthy patron of architectural taste. As it will be seen, I was too pessimistic; but soon after the war little could be done except from a position inside officialdom, a lesson cruelly underlined, when, in conjunction with a charming and valued client, I attempted to demonstrate how post-war building might be carried out.

Before the war, for this ideal client I had developed the Manor House and grounds at Cornwell in Oxfordshire. Hitler's brutal intervention brought our blissful architectural honeymoon to an abrupt end. When all our vain imaginings had been stowed away in cold storage, she gave over the whole splendid creation to the Red Cross as a hospital 'for the duration', and herself gallantly plunging into strenuous and responsible war jobs far more hazardous than any that came my hum-drum way. She survived unscathed, and with her architectural appetite apparently sharpened by abstinence, she felt impelled to buy up most of the whole town of Littlehampton in order to transform what was then a bit of a sow's ear into something a little more like a silk purse.

A gracious new neighbourhood of seemly working-class houses was generously planned as part of the new deal, and I took the whole scheme proudly along to show Aneurin Bevan, the newly appointed Minister of Health, to get his necessary official blessing. Nothing could have been warmer than his welcome (we were old friends anyhow) but NO—the new government policy must be rigidly adhered to and *all* such housing must be carried out by Local Authorities *only*, without any competition from private enterprise of any sort, no matter how well-designed or generously intended. It seemed to me pretty silly, and I said so—but there it was, and there were *we*—a stack of lovely surveys and plans—an enthusiastic explanatory meeting behind us, but nothing to show for it all beyond a bit of face-lifting here and there and the rehabilitation and general up-grading of the town's rather formidable main hotel with Lionel Brett,[1] for which Hans Feibusch painted a most spirited great mural.

Perhaps the most useful by-product of my consultations with Nye Bevan was his agreeing to lower the by-law height for rooms from eight feet to seven foot six, for which I had long agitated, arguing that what mattered was not space over our heads, but on our floors, where we (not being bats) lived. I had anyhow tirelessly pressed for this reform on architectural grounds— isolated little houses would have better exterior proportions and would 'stick up' less bleakly.

Baulked of her intended municipal rescue work, my frustrated patron sold out and went to live in one of the two successive houses she built for herself in the South of France. Insofar as she was my architectural pupil, I never had a better, nor a brighter, and I like to think that she still regards me as 'cher maitre'. Apart from her purpose-built French houses, my paragon had many other interests and connections in various parts of the world. She eventually decided that her English estate was rather 'surplus to requirements' and that she wouldn't really have much use for it. Asking me what she should do with it, I

[1] Now Viscount Esher, Rector of the Royal College of Art.

suggested: 'Why not give it all to the National Trust? It would be exactly their cup of tea.' 'Good idea, splendid,' she said, 'I'll run around and look at some of their properties and see how they maintain them.' Returning from this inspection she said, 'No— none of their gardens are maintained as they should be and I want to make sure mine *are*.'

Of course this was grossly unfair as most war-time gardens had little to show beyond potato crops and lawns become hay-fields, whereas she, up to the war, had kept a dozen or so gardeners busy under a really expert and enthusiastic young head. I had rashly warned the Trust to stand by for a notable windfall, and when I confessed this to the now non-donor, she exclaimed, 'Oh dear! I hate disappointing them, what can I do?' I replied that a suitable cheque might cheer them up—and that she sent, a very handsome one. As to the place itself, she gave it, or sold it cheap (I dont't know which) to one of her many old friends, whom she felt she could confidently trust to keep the place as she had kept it, and from all I hear, she chose well.

Rebuffed in my first effort at post-war rebuilding, when Sam (later Lord) Silkin offered me the job of chairing the committee for the first New Town, Stevenage, I jumped at the chance. Mine was an instinctive and impulsive appointment on Mr. Silkin's part—he had come to Portmeirion on his characteristically thorough reconnaissance of North Wales as part of the National Estate, for which he had become responsible, and I had been his guide. I suppose he thought 'Here is an enterprising fellow, full of town and country planning enthusiasm, and even some experience—mightn't he be helpful?' So that when, some months later, we quite accidentally were walking towards each other in the House of Commons, he greeted me with 'How would you like to be Chairman of my first New Town Corpora-tion?'—my response, naturally, a startled and rapturous 'Nothing better'.

We, the first of his New Town committees, were tremen-dously excited by the whole idea, and strained at the leash to be off in full cry. There was plenty of hostility to face and overcome, both nationally and locally, and I rather relished the role of 'counsel for the defence' on platforms, on radio and in the press.

I quote from a broadcast I made at that time, which shows what were our hopes, and gives an idea of our excitement and intoxication at this chance to set a sorely needed standard of urbanity to the whole country:

> It is our aim to build a town where some sixty thousand people, all sorts of different people, can live together, happily and graciously and prosperously, which means that we have, first, to be thinking all the time in terms of actual living human beings. Roads and houses, buildings of all kinds indeed everything we do being only the means to satisfying their needs.
>
> A town fit to live in. Our first job is to set the task for our technicians and so to guide them, so to foresee what is wanted and generally to shape policy, that we can get for our citizens, present and future, whom we have been appointed to represent, what most of them seem most to need—a place in which they can feel warmly and intimately at home. Can that be done? Why ever not?
>
> This time the citizens, through us their agents, are going to take charge right from the very beginning, and we are together planning things, with nobody's interests or reasonable desires left out, but with the welfare of the whole community paramount.
>
> Of course we are guided by the accepted principles of planning, but we must apply them to our particular area imaginitively, making use of every natural feature, hill or valley, wood or water, every happy accident of every sort. Not just imposing some theoretical, mechanical lay-out on our delightfully diversified countryside. By welcoming nature as our planning partner, we hope to attain grace as well as efficiency—real efficiency, which means a whole lot more than just good traffic, communications, well-placed factories and first-rate public services. Those we take for granted as only the bare beginnings of what we are out for. It means providing, and generously, for all the needs we can of men, women and children of all sorts and ages, spiritually and physically, at work and at leisure, throughout the whole town which is to be their home. One of these needs, we believe, is beauty.
>
> Now efficiency means industry, factories (of course smokeless) tidily grouped together, away but easily reached from people's homes, handy for rail sidings, yet with restaurants, recreation grounds and gardens along with them, for those who do not want to get home for the dinner break. It means getting these industries well balanced, giving not only variety of choice and interest, but of

employment too, as between men and women and beginners, the highly skilled and the not so highly skilled. Indeed, balance is the aim right through from education and the social services, zoning and road plans, to the proportioning of open spaces to built-up areas, of drains and water supplies, of theatres, churches, shops, cinemas, libraries, clinics and pubs to population. And even of this section of the population to that, of hand-workers to head-workers, of trades to professions, of the weekly wage earners to the salaried, and so forth. . . .

The New Towns—first under the development corporations, then under their own municipalities—will be their own landlords, in the interests of their own citizens. No single building will ever be allowed to trespass beyond the line marked as the town's settled and permanent boundary. There can be no claim jumping, no enclosures, no squatting, no sudden and horrid surprises—the first country cow will always rub her sides against the same last urban lamp-post.

After a while, such dreamings looked less and less realistic, my fondly imagined New Town withdrew further and further into the distance as slow-motion intervened, and we had to deal with such mundane questions as how best to contrive that all our sewage outfall should reach the River Lea and quench the thirst of London. The long-drawn out preliminaries that stood between us and any visible results were barely launched before we were overtaken by the looming economic crises, and all our fine imaginings were whittled down to a more or less token demonstration that this new seed had indeed germinated and had *not* been eaten by mice.

Successively the other new corporations were launched under such seasoned civil servants as Lord Reith, Sir Ernest Gowers and so on, leaving me, the trial ball as it were, the only amateur. As I am highly allergic to committees and paper-work generally, I felt increasingly frustrated with the minimal bread and butter building in immediate prospect. I soon realized that, as an administrator, I was no match for my experienced fellow chairmen, and it was a real relief when my minister, Mr. Silkin, agreed and very kindly sacked me, with the most cordial good wishes on both sides.

The passing of Silkin's 1947 Town and Country Planning Act had really seemed at the time to bring with it a whiff of

sanity. Much of the Act is now out of date, and has been found
to be ineffective, inapplicable or even actually mischievous, and
it clearly needs radical revision and extension in the light of
experience, as of course do most Acts, however intelligently
framed and skilfully drafted. Such revisions do not come of themselves. They have to be clamoured for long and loudly by those
who know and care and by as many others as ever they can
persuade to clamour with them. For Parliament, which is ever-
lastingly hemmed in by importunate pressure groups of all sorts
lobbying for this or that, is apt just to listen politely and do nothing
whatsoever. Nearly fifty years ago I wrote:

> The time has come for those who care about amenity to hitch their
> wagon to a political policy, if not indeed to a party—those who have
> ever given election-time help at committee rooms will recall the
> miscellaneous sort of pressures to which a candidate is subjected.
> Both the temperance party and the brewing interest wish to be
> positively assured of his soundness on the liquor question; others
> interested, it may be, in Prayer Book reform or in farming, wish to
> know whether he favours the use of chasuble in the first case or a
> bounty on sugar beet in the second. Our legislators undoubtedly
> gauge the relative importance of political questions, both local and
> imperial, by the amount of fuss their constituents make about them
> at election time, whilst the public in their turn forms its notions of
> priority from the prominence given to various subjects in politics and
> consequently in the media.

The difficulty today is to find a ready answer to our problems,
when as so often happens, fashionable cures seem in turn to give
rise to fresh diseases. The air becomes thick with the sociological
philosophies of contending groups and splinter groups. Lewis
Mumford has long been pointing out the dangers of our New
Towns and housing estates, but it was Michael Young in his book
Family and Kinship in East London, who threw something of a
bombshell among us town planners. After years of living and
close contacts and study in Bethnal Green, his final conclusion
broadly was that there is a very great deal to be said for the
tight-packed integration even of the typical slum, as against the
loose-knit, fragmented housing estate which, he held, bears

little relation to the real needs of human society, the actual unit of which is *not* that of just parents and children as planners have commonly assumed, but a three or even four tier affair, including grandparents and grandchildren with all sorts of ramifications through uncles and aunts on both sides, the 'Extended Family' as he calls it, around the dominant Matriarchal figure of 'Mum', that ties in at its edges with a whole complex of familiar friends and close neighbours that in turn tie in with other 'Extended Families' to form a very real, conscious, cohesive and active neighbourhood. To produce, preserve or foster this traditional and desirable state of things, Dr. Young, being wiser than most, sees a favourable architectural lay-out as essential and asserts that we have thus far failed to find it. As Lewis Mumford points out: 'We have been betrayed into planning for motor cars instead of for men'—or words to that effect—whilst Sir Hugh Casson has been saying: 'Let us face the facts—be realistic—we have now to plan no longer for soft little animals pottering around on their own two legs, but for hard steel canisters hurtling about with these same little animals inside them.'

So where are we? It is at times impossibly difficult to tell. I have been caught out myself when, in the course of a tour of inspection, Lady Simon showed me round the then burgeoning Withenshore development, which I found immensely heartening; it appeared to be embodying so many of the ideas that seemed to me essential to civilized urban living. Provide a generous, well-planned, seemly, humane setting, I had always maintained, and you will get an appreciative, co-operative, and thoroughly civilized citizenry. I was a bit shaken then, when, revisiting the place as a member of the Trunk Roads Advisory Committee for the Ministry of Transport, I found that it was proposed to *enclose* the elegant open footbridge spanning the main roads to prevent the youth of the place hurling bottles and even old bedsteads on to passing cars. That a little undermined my faith in the civilizing effect of good surroundings on conduct, but not fundamentally for, I reflected, had the surroundings been barbarous, it might have been bombs instead of bottles and bedsteads. One learns to be patient and not to expect too much, too soon, and to realize that good architecture, well-thought out planning and a gracious setting generally are only contributory and not in themselves enough, though it's all that I have personally striven for, on the principle of 'every man to his last'. I still believe that our New Towns, with all their faults, have helped to prevent the frustrations and disfigurements of our larger cities from becoming infinitely worse than in fact they are.

3

The British Meteor—1951

The great event of the post-war years which filled us with hope for the revival of British Architecture, the joyous exception to all the penny wise, pound foolishness of the government building programmes of the following decades, with their disastrous and de-humanising effects, was the Festival of Britain of 1951. This imaginative forward-looking show so brilliantly mounted on the South Bank by a team of avant-garde architects recruited by Sir Hugh Casson in a mood of gay adventure, really did come off.

Of the Battersea Pleasure Gardens I wrote at the time:

> It is not easy to catch its sprightly elegance and entrap it in a phrase. It is easier to hazard its sources of inspiration from Xanadu to Eglinton, from Harun-al-Raschid to Lord George Sanger, from the Brighton Pavilion to the Tivoli Gardens at Rome and their frolicsome namesake at Copenhagen. There are conscious hints of Vauxhall, Ranelagh and Cremorne in so-named commemorative beer gardens, of the gay baroque palace of Heilbrun—birthday surprise of a Prince Archbishop of Salzburg for his mistress—where pretty garden toys worked by tumbling water tinkle out the music of Mozart.

There is also more than a hint of the Mad Hatter and the Pied Piper (as there was also in the Lion and Unicorn Pavilion on the South Bank), of Monk Lewis and Heath Robinson, which is merely to say that those we have to thank for this astonishing gallopade (astonishing it is and thank them we should) are all highly civilized and literate persons on such easy and intimate terms with beauty of every kind that they can be witty and jolly about it and laugh at it all, as also of course at themselves. In place of the correct and classical formality that one might have feared in a government-sponsored Command Junket, in place of the 'Ghastly Good Taste' lampooned by John Betjeman, we were given an exhuberant laughing fancy, a bubbling prodigality of the rococo, with the opposite dangers of the arch and the whimsical almost equally and happily avoided. Almost, but not quite. There are, to be sure, the Peter Pan and Emmet railways, but there is also a superb Emmet aeroplane. The few concessions made to popular sentimentality are justified, indeed essential in such a show.

What is really entrancing is the reflection that the whole of this gigantic joke was ordained by Parliament, and (if indirectly) 'run from Whitehall' at the government's expense, which (Oh, we know) is the taxpayers', yours and ours, which again is why the Calamity Howlers so furiously raged together. This is, however, just precisely one of the things we had always hoped that a government would one day do—act the princely patron of the outdoor visual arts on a reasonably large scale. The cost may have been considerable, but this thing was worth it, showing as it has that we can create beauty without solemnity, and, when made, not merely respect it, but enjoy it as naturally as we do witty talk or a glass of good beer.

Possibly a little more high-level architectural discipline and co-ordination at the top would have made all this fizzing invention even more telling, by securing proper scale and a just proportion between the several parts, without in any way cramping all the spontaneity. It might also have organized the actual works and time-and-progress schedules better and so made the cost-accounts less dismal reading.

But, being used to spending vastly greater sums for projects that are no sort of fun at all, we have enjoyed this lovely toy as the treat it is, an instructional toy that seems to have done us all sorts of good.

I hoped that all this was the beginning of an exciting new movement in the Architecture of Pleasure and in Architecture generally—sadly it all too soon revealed itself as the finale. Some part of its influence lingered on in the Coronation decorations in London, and to some extent in the 'popular' art of Carnaby Street fashions of the 1960s, but of the more serious architectural teaching, the lesson was not learnt, not even in the further development of the South Bank.

The one permanent memorial is the L.C.C.'s Royal Festival Hall, and as such deserves our attention. To begin with, the unfestive of London were sanctimoniously shocked by the extravagance of building any such thing, the whole venture being crossly called 'This incredible monument to the folly and false pride of a cult of long-haired aesthetes'. Actually its architects, Sir Robert Mathew (who sketched many of the preliminary plans on his knee in our own little sitting room, while staying with us) and Sir Leslie Martin, wore their hair quite short, and what they, with the L.C.C. behind them, succeeded in doing was to produce in an incredibly short time, not only an astonishingly efficient auditorium in which music can really be heard by a large audience, but also a building from the rest of whose interior—foyers, staircases, balconies, roof-gardens, restaurants, and so on—the most flattering views of London and her river can be enjoyed.

It was in a world darkened by doubt and danger that this great work, dedicated to the arts of peace, valiantly rose. Any too luxuriant flowering would certainly have been felt by the sensitive as inappropriate and unacceptable at the time. Magnanimity, spaciousness, technical and functional perfection, and quality, yes; but any ostentatious swagger, and display of opulence, any too esoteric flights of fancy, no. Whence, partly, its general character: its basic structure has been finely and closely conditioned by its site and by its function, which last is to constitute a *popular* cultural centre where—as it might be—the ordinary citizen can get to know the world of music as part of a jolly and generally stimulating night-out.

As to the site, it is not merely London's best, but one of the world's most notable, facing as it does (from its blunt promontory on the Thames' South Bank) an arc of unexpected civic splendour across the river that is unequalled anywhere. Till Mathew and Martin displayed it to us, few Londoners had any idea how grandly their city and its river showed from here. Indeed the fact is that they were scarcely to be seen at all. The Royal Festival Hall gave us a worthy belvedere from which to survey a matchless panorama across the wide and moving river. Those who have any doubts about its exterior looks should judge it by actually using it, and thus appraise it by the standards of Free Architecture, which were those of its designers.

However, whilst freely allowing that the Hall has all the major virtues to be expected of a large, modern, national building, it may, nonetheless, be held to lack certain minor graces and elegancies which might be looked for in a temple of the arts. Within, those who feel that music and colour have a certain subtle relationship are likely to find the interiors of the hall generally somewhat lacking in warmth, intimacy, and detailed interest. Particularly do the great windows looking to the river seem somewhat stark and cold without rich and colourful curtains and to cry aloud for generous draping. Again, why no sparkling lustrous chandeliers? . . . No mirrors in which we may catch their glitter, and also secretly admire ourselves in gala-dress or scrutinize our fellows by reflection and so without offence?

I will confess a nostalgic weakness myself for the shadowed privacy of the traditional box as the very symbol of gilded and softly upholstered luxury—an appropriate bower for the necessary digestive interlude between dinner at old Romano's and supper at the Grand Babylon, with transport, of course, by private hansom. Even from the pit I liked simply to behold these cosily glowing little booths with their fully jewelled and often decorative tenants, high-life tableaux vivants about whose members one might speculate agreeably. In short, I am of the fleshly Walter Sickert school in this matter of theatre decor, for scarlet and gold as against beige austerity, for sparkling chandeliers against fluorescent tubes, for an exuberant fancy even, rather than a too reasonable or reproachful restraint.

For me, at least, any concert or indeed any public performance of any kind is definitely in the way of a treat, a gala occasion, a 'night out', and to be perfectly happy I do need the architecture to conform to and reflect, and so enhance, my festival mood. Had the garden setting and the attendant trees been allowed to adorn the terrace more fully, and those few 'petits soins' been granted, some sculpture perhaps, or some tapestry, to alleviate the stark interior, I would have grown more used to its air of bland detachment, but they have not, and nor have I. The area of concrete has indeed spread, without softening, all along this stretch of river, and the newly completed National Theatre I find indeed a hard lump to swallow. Here, too, the note should have been one of gaiety, instead of which we have a fortress-like building, forbidding and reproachful rather than inviting.

However I really have no ear for music. I cannot say that I have used the Festival Hall enough to be won over to it on grounds other than architectural, except for once when I believe it must have been the exhilarating atmosphere both of the Hall and of the Festival as a whole which so moved me. A huge orchestra under Sir Malcolm Sargent, as it were, 'played in' the new concert chamber on its opening night. I don't remember the programme whatever it was, and one's exaltation was no doubt chiefly due to the occasion itself, the triumphant completion of a great cultural monument against all the crippling odds of the war's aftermath. Amabel and I were there not as musical connoisseurs, nor as loyally supporting the Royal Presence, but simply as close friends of the late Sir Robert Mathew, chief architect of the whole great complex, and I as author of the descriptive and illustrated *Record* that I had written against time to be available for this Royal and gala first night. I suppose it was all this keyed-up, tip-toe exaltation that somehow loosened something or other in my otherwise musically unresponsive brain, so that when 'Rule Britannia' crashed out under Sir Malcolm's baton, I felt my scalp bristling and tears actually coursing down my cheeks, the final 'God Save the Queen' being almost equally un-manning. To many of us it seemed a triumphal occasion, but those threadbare old tunes are scarcely great music, and anyway, what does poor old Britannia rule now?

4

Great Expectations

Allergic to committees of any sort as I have ever been, it has nonetheless been my fate to be sucked into a wide variety of such, nearly all concerned more or less with amenity matters, town planning, countryside protection, National Parks, The National Trust, Preservation Councils, Civic Societies and all sorts of similar bodies for promoting or protecting or preventing this or that. I have as a propagandist always greatly preferred field work or journalism to the tedium of the necessary routine executive meetings which was only slightly mitigated when I happened to be chairman. I am afraid it is my innate impatience that makes me so poor and reluctant a committee man, and the hours spent in conference the slowest to pass in all my life.

Some official jobs were less frustrating than others, and definitely less so than Stevenage had been. I was appointed to the 'Advisory Committee on the Landscape Treatment of Trunk Roads' set up by Lord Watkinson when Minister of Transport. A large part of our work consisted of reconnaissance on the actual site of proposed or current road works, from the Scottish

border down to South Wales and Cornwall, interspersed with
more or less regular monthly meetings at the Ministry, where we
conferred with its officials. Of course we had no say in the shaping
of major policy. Our role was mostly concerned with such details
as tree planting, the treatment of embankments and cuttings, the
preservation or provision of anything that could enhance the
scenic amenity for drivers, obscure eyesores and generally
mitigate and civilize the inevitable crudities of large-scale public
works.

First under the chairmanship of the late Sir David Bowes-Lyon
and then, on his death, under Sir Eric Savill (of the Savill
Gardens, Windsor) and finally Sir George Taylor, Director of
Kew Gardens, the Committee represented a wide variety of
experience: arboriculture, horticulture, landscaping, forestry,
architecture, surveying, agriculture and such, it submitted its
successive reports and suggestions, and that these were listened to
and usually implemented was what made our efforts so unusually
worthwhile. Mrs. Barbara Castle, as Minister of Transport, took
particular interest in our efforts to help and guide her officials and
engineers, and indeed suggested the publication of a little book
describing our activities that I wrote for the Ministry, to which
she added her own introduction for official publication by
H.M.S.O.

It was all most exciting and stimulating: to fly in a helicopter
along the proposed route of the first of our motorways, the M1,
as I did, seemed at the time ever so advanced and future-looking,
but already that great and ingeniously constructed 'speedway' is
regarded as technically 'old-hat'. Indeed one of the most interesting things about this work was the realization of how quickly
changes in methods of transport have taken place. My grandfather, and his grandfather before him, had always ridden up to
Cambridge on horseback, selling their ponies when they got
there. I myself had driven through villages on the borders of
England and Wales where the inhabitants had never before seen
a motor car. It seems hard to believe now. My attendance record
with this Ministry Highways Committee was my best ever, and I
soldiered faithfully and indeed zealously on under the three
successive chairmen. I only dismissed myself when I was able to

recruit *two* new and eager members to fill my place: Bodfan Gruffyd, the landscapist, and Bruno de Hamel, the well-known photographer. De Hamel is acutely landscape conscious, and has lately produced a book, much grander than mine, on the Ministry's road-planning and building activities.

Directly after the Second War, I seemed to be considered a 'natural' for all sorts of committees and enquiries, largely I suppose because I did not seem very obviously fully stretched in any very meaningful national effort—which was, frustratingly, true enough. So I was pushed onto the pretty representative Committee appointed to advise on Welsh reconstruction after the war. Our meetings were held in Cardiff, far less accessible in wartime than was London, and my journeys thither and back were sufficiently trying to make me feel that I must, somehow, be an actual cog in the great national machine. The results of our deliberations were duly published in an impressive 'Report' and although we were certainly out in some of our pronouncements, we were right on target in others.

My next governmental chore was the chairing of the Committee appointed to enquire into and report on the British Glass Industry into which I was relentlessly pushed by my old friend Stafford Cripps, despite my protestations that I knew nothing whatever about the trade, as the surprised professionals would soon discover; he refused to take 'no' as my answer and there I was. We had been colleagues together in various ploys involving propaganda for improved design and assuredly that was what the Glassmakers most manifestly lacked; I was clearly being set at them to promote just that.

The glass firm's then prevailing idea of excellence was a flawless metal of the utmost transparency and clarity, cut to ribbons in intricate geometrical patterns—admittedly requiring great skill, but producing—what? I scandalized the proud producers of these elaborately and expensively manufactured wares by professing my own preference for the natural simplicity of the jolly great flagons and beakers of clouded glass, full of bubbles, presumably foreign imports, still being sold at sixpence a time. Delegations went to America and of course to Sweden in pursuit of helpful evidence, and our fat Report was duly published with my own minority squeaks but, I would judge, with no great effect.

For a long time I had been writing and speaking about country-side conservation and public access, as well as nature reserves, so that when John Dower's miraculously comprehensive Report, commissioned by the government, appeared I was deemed an obvious choice for the Hobhouse Committee set up to study the whole question of National Parks and report after a thorough country-wide reconnaissance. At first we worked from maps and met in London, but as we made up our list of likely candidates for National Park status, we held meetings within their various borders, for a more thorough examination, and discussions with knowledgeable natives. On these occasions we were often hospitably entertained by sympathetic local landowners with large houses, as though we were an amateur theatrical group, which added a very agreeable aspect to the job. In one large and rambling castle in South Wales, whose owner was only too delighted to make his home of use to a wider public, we found we were not the only guests, although we were a party of at least a dozen: a group from the Fleet Air Arm was accommodated in another wing!

Pretty well every interest involved was thoroughly covered, from our Chairman, Sir Henry Hobhouse, a West Country liberal landowner experienced in local government affairs, through Sir Julian Huxley and Major Buxton and other specialist naturalists, geologists, ecologists, agriculturalists and forestry experts, to Lord Chorley for legal guidance, and so on. I was supposed to represent landscape, architectural and coastal interests generally, at the same time acting more or less as member for Wales, my own habitat Snowdonia being second only to the Lake District in order of seniority of the ten Parks finally established. I had in fact, years earlier, involved myself in the National Parks effort by buying a mountain ridge looking across Lake Gwynant at Snowdon, and giving it, in order to preserve its virgin integrity, to the National Trust with the expressed hope that it might prove to be the nucleus around which some sort of Snowdonian National Park might solidify, as it ultimately did.

This property of Hafod Llwyfog has provided me with the

c

means for a Machiavellian plot, a spot of shock therapy, in the cause of my long-standing battle against the barbarity of out-door advertising that in the early 1930s was casting its disfiguring blight across the countryside without any control whatsoever. Any farmer with a gap in his roadside fence that needed making stock-proof could invite any thrusting advertiser with a hoarding or a large enamelled iron sign to fill it for him and pay him for the privilege—or stick his stuff on barn doors, or even stencil his message on their roofs or, indeed, do almost anything anywhere that did not physically impede traffic on the highway. Prodding the government to forbid or even curb this barbarity had produced nothing but faint sympathetic noises and I felt both desperate and helpless, when I had what seemed to be an inspiration. I would offer, free, to the most flagrant advertisers an already celebrated background from which they could cry their wares as raucously as they pleased across Lake Gwynant and up and down the valley, and to all who passed along the scenic highway between Beddgelert and Bettws-y-Coed. What would meet their eyes instead of the green mount against the background of lake and crags, would be a pyramid of blistering multi-coloured eyesores shouting down the ancient peace and serenity that had reigned there time out of mind—probably for millennia.

I would, in short, promote and abet such a spectacular outrage that a commensurate reaction must surely follow—even from the somnolent government—legislation be quickly introduced and urgently passed lest public fury take over and a nationwide 'Battle of the Billboards' lead on to more than merely material violence. Then, as I was hatching the details of my horrid and desperate plot, there came a gleam of sanity and hope. The Government, prodded by a coalition of now thoroughly aroused amenity bodies and dedicated individuals, at last firmly promised effective control and, what is more, kept its word, so that the creeping leprosy of out-door advertising was at last stayed, and we may hope finally extirpated for ever. This belated relief was, of course, doubly welcome to me personally, as not only was our cause won but I was spared the odium that must inevitably otherwise have attached to me for my apparently treacherous desertion to the enemy. I confidently expected eager bites from all the most

pushing advertisers who had proved their ruthless and uninhibited enterprise elsewhere, hawking bicycles, baby-foods,
patent medicines, soaps, distempers, inks, pens, petrol or whatever. They would enjoy this free and prestigious privilege for at
least a year, and thereafter, still free, by the half-year, until the
privilege might be withdrawn owing to 'unforeseen circumstances'.

So, as I have said, I gave the 'Snowdon View' ridge to the
National Trust, and the old Plâs and the rest of the property to
our daughter Charlotte, married and settled in New Zealand
with a family of five—so that they should still have their own
roots in Wales. All I have kept as an outlying island of my own
Brondanw Estate is the green mount at the lake head—site of the
epic battle that never was. If ever Wales, or some heroic son (or
daughter) of Wales achieved some signal triumph deserving
national celebration, I feel that here is our little Mount Olympus,
that could be most fittingly crowned by a suitably rugged tower or
columned commemorative temple. I feel that it eagerly awaits
such coronation—sure sign that the conservationist has not quite
buried the architect!

When I had drawn up a proposed scheme for the Snowdonian
Park, I showed it to my colleagues who immediately inquired why
I had put the boundary precisely where I had, with a small
digression to include my own Croesor Valley. I reminded them
that one of the obligations laid upon us was to ensure the welfare
of the local fauna, among which I judged myself to be! I drew a
circle excluding Blaenau Ffestiniog however, as an area of non-
amenity directly opposed to the principles of the National Parks,
and also excluded the coast around Portmeirion, but for a rather
different reason! I was convinced that the Trust I had myself set
up would look after it better than any government-controlled
body could hope to do, and I still believe it can. Altogether the
whole procedure of inspecting, discussing, assessing and finalising
our report, with reasons for our recommendations, took at least
two years, and I think that, apart from the Trunk Roads Committee, I never spent so long a time on any job more enjoyably or
perhaps more usefully.

Have the National Parks been a success? The answer is undoubtedly Yes. Of course they are not all that their ardent partisans could have wished, but how much, much better than none at all! In a country so care-less of its heritage as this, it was a miracle that somehow, we got them established at all, and not at all surprising that it should all have been done as meanly as possible and that the whole Park administration should have been consistently starved of funds from birth. As a result, they can't do much in the way of 'enhancing' the amenities and natural beauties of their territories, one of the duties laid upon them in their Charter; nor have they been able to set up a central fund, for which I had strongly pressed, from which subventions could, where necessary, be paid to cover the difference in cost between ordinarily acceptable building and the higher standard appropriate to the status of the National Parks. They can hardly do anything positive, yet even a negative watchfulness is something; the prevention, through planning control, of petty discourtesies or real outrages is all gain. The original hope of areas of special distinction where special architectural good manners are expected from all who live or work or visit within their boundaries have for the most part been borne out, the fears of the Calamity Howlers proven as so often over pessimistic.

These fears, of insensitive trampling and despoiling, held by farmers and naturalists and people who wished for wildness inviolate, had this time, in fact, a basis in truth. With the overwhelming mass of our teeming population town-bred, barbarously reared in far from splendid cities, having little contact with beauty of any kind and, therefore, knowing or caring little for it, the introduction was a hazardous one. For one is unlikely to respond appropriately when presented with the hitherto unknown. Yet, it was a risk that had to be taken. We had to put up with the inevitable misunderstandings and gaucheries that marked the first contacts of the uninitiated with the hitherto unrealised heritage, of the multitudes with out solitudes. In order that the very heritage itself be spared, and not dissolve utterly away at this unaccustomed touch, this overdue presentation had assuredly to be made. It was altogether too dangerous that the vast majority of its heirs should be insensitive to its loveliness, without pride in its possession and careless of its preservation.

A wide popularity and appreciation; a democratic good will, an alert public opinion that would protect them from injury and maintain their integrity against the Philistine for our possibly more civilized successors, had somehow to be assured. The National Parks and their younger brothers, the Areas of Outstanding Natural Beauty, have gone a long way to fulfilling this task; they have helped in popularizing the enjoyment of their beauty by making lovely buildings and lovely places generally accessible, without somehow thereby impairing their distinctive characters.

5

A Criss-cross Reconnaissance

As, from the title of this book, the reader will be expecting detailed accounts of my travels to all corners of the earth, I will now attempt somewhat to fulfil this obligation. The circuit is necessarily incomplete however, since my journeys to Russia, Scandinavia, New Zealand and Australia, the Middle East and my remote control contacts with China, have all been dealt with already in my earlier autobiography *Architect Errant*, but I do feel that I am able to say and, on challenge, prove that I have at one time or another visited most parts of the world.

Since in the mid-50s controls on private building still left me with little work, and travel to parts of the sterling area was not restricted as it was elsewhere, we set off to tour the Caribbean. It is, of course, the Caribbean's fortunate climate from which all its other blessings flow—the trade-wind-conditioned tropics. Encouraged by the warm sea, the coral polyps have there built up their labyrinthine reefs, where dandified tropical fish now astonish the new species of goggle-eyed divers far more than they are themselves surprised. Surf-pounded coral rock strews the shores of lagoons and sheltered bays with their fine sand, a band of white between the rich green of palm, sea grape and mangrove, and the ultra-marine of the shallow sea. Back of the coastal fringe there may be more or less indigenous bush, lush and complex, or cultivated crops, both varying within a certain range, not only from island to island, but from cape to cape, according to local variations of soil and aspect, custom and local economy.

True, in Barbados ('blood-curdlingly genteel' as Patrick Leigh-Fermor—whom we travelled back with—unkindly called it) the great expanses of sugar cane can be a little wearisome, whilst arrowroot on St. Vincent and cotton anywhere, or for that matter yams or even pineapple are scenically frankly rather dull. But coconut palms, banana, cocoa and coffee and, above all, the citrus and breadfruit trees, all these if intermixed as they generally are, give a most lively and becoming mantle to the cultivated lands. In the bush, particularly where it becomes high forest, the variety of handsome timber trees is great—teak and mahogany, silk-cotton tree and banyan; the heavy rainfall that forests enjoy being found on the high mountain peaks that give so many of the islands an exciting silhouette. North of the Jamaican ranges around Ocho Rios, alongside all the tropical luxuriance, one is surprised to find large cattle ranches with herds of Indian and European cross-breds grazing savannas studded with fine spreading trees, all very much like an English park, especially when the presiding Great House forms part of the picture.

Bad times for sugar meant bad times for nearly all Great Houses on nearly all the islands, and too many of them have fallen to ruin, or near ruin, or have totally disappeared. Rose Hall on Jamaica had a spine-chilling criminal record and an alleged very active haunting to set against its architectural distinction and as some excuse for its recent wrecking; but Farley Hill, the finest old Great House on Barbados, is deserted and derelict simply because it is too large and too remote from the sea and town and other amenities to survive as such, though it seemed a tragedy if no use could be found for so noble a building before it was too late. For although in Bridgetown and elsewhere on the island there are here and there attractive Georgian remnants, there is little enough of architectural merit to relieve the prevailing blight of mediocrity and worse that even the Caribbean has not escaped.

The new promise of better standards apparent throughout the islands is particularly encouraging, from the Palladian coral-rock elegance of Geoffrey Jellicoe's marine pavilion for Ronald Tree (a tribute to the Villa Malcontenta on the Brenta) and the Works Department's new public buildings—both on Barbados—to Mr. Lewis's Catholic Church at Port-of-Spain, and Mr. Ward's lively exploitation of his well-guarded Mill Reef territory on Antigua, where the luxurious demands of his select American Clientele and the fabulous setting of little capes and coral lagoons are both brilliantly served by his imaginative modernism. Indeed it is such a setting and such a climate and perhaps even such a purpose (that of seaside holiday buildings) that seem to give free domestic architecture its full scope and justification. Its open planning and its informal give-and-take between in-doors and out-of-doors is ideal under such conditions and is not the embarrassing make-believe that it can sometimes be with us. The same intelligent adaptation to site, climate and function is also apparent in the newer coastal clubs and hotels that are such important dollar-earners throughout the Caribbean, even Jamaica's Montego Bay (which one had feared to find a sort of millionaires' Blackpool) in fact exploiting both its happy situation as a tropical *plage* and its prosperous clientele, not without gaiety and even good sense. Certainly it is expensive, which alas goes for most of the islands, so that with the long flight or voyage out and back, a West Indian holiday must remain a rare treat for the Briton.

Nonetheless, tourism is becoming more and more important in the still difficult economy of many islands where basic agricultural production is only here and there supplemented by the working of oil or bauxite or by light industry. The imbalance of population and means of livelihood is of course reflected in the embarrassing influx of West Indians into Britain and the newly independent states have still to find the right answers to a lot of pressing questions, not only economic. West Indian skills and products generally are, for the most part, too alike to foster much inter-island trade, and partly for that very reason intercommunication even between near neighbours used to be tenuous and uncertain in the extreme.

I believe that the growth of tourism has at least encouraged a reliable inter-island air service. Twenty-five years ago, one was forced into all sorts of ingenuities and shifts to get about. We resorted to island schooners, sloops, launches, amphibians, even rowing boats. This meant that our itinerary became very much a matter of hand-to-mouth opportunism with plenty of surprise land-falls never envisaged or even heard of before one actually got amongst the islands. Which, being assuredly mostly gain, did necessarily mean that some of our intended destinations were never reached at all. . . .

Aircraft were grounded, airstrips reported out of order, schooners delayed, motor launches changed their schedule, necessitating sudden switches of plan resulting, as often as not, in our finding ourselves somewhere quite other than expected, and probably more interesting. Thus did we find ourselves most agreeably delivered to Union Island, Grenada, Becuia and St. Vincent, instead of to Dominica, with Monserrat and the Virgin Islands finally abandoned. So did we get unintended glimpses, too, of Puerto Rico and Hispaniola and three uncovenanted calls at small Jamaican ports on our returning banana boat on which we had the luck to find the Philip Hugh-Joneses[1] as shipmates. In short, on our Caribbean journey, we failed to see all that we had planned to see, but a great deal more than had ever entered our heads, or that travel agents wot of.

Certainly we found this part of the world was as interesting as any, bristling with problems which, if greater elsewhere, are nowhere so readily observable. We drew comparisons (often mistaken) between the British, French and other Islands, mourned over the ruins of St. Pierre, rejoiced over the eleventh-hour rescue of Nelson's English Harbour and its resuscitation as a bustling yacht-yard and cruising base, and were charmed by the Regency amenities of St. George's as well as grieved by their neglect. We admired Trinidad's modern oil concerns, models of streamlined industrial elegance—(NOT so her dismal pitch lake),

---

[1] Philip Hugh-Jones, the physician and explorer, and his wife Hilary.

her fine agricultural institute, her steel bands and calypso singers. We also approved of Jamaica's West Indian University on the Vigunea Plain, ten miles from Kingston, where the architects Norman and Dawbarn have given it most gracious functional shape. So much to see and hear and ponder and remember. We made informing contacts of all sorts, West Indian, American and European, official and other—idyllic tropical landscapes, miserable peasant habitations, bouncing wide-eyed children, friendly people. . . .

Things will have changed since our visit, but the sea is still the same—if you have an aqualung or a snorkel with you, beware! You will find that more and more you spend the glowing days head under in the warm shallows of the coral reefs getting on terms with a radiance of submarine life still new to most of us. So visitors are likely to return with perhaps fewer statistics than they should, but with Oh! what memories of beauty—and with what a tan!

Fortunately we had friends to stay with on Barbados and on the, to us, most alluring of all the islands, Little Bequi, we found the Brownlows[1] at what was then its only, but most civilized, little hotel, on their way to their own splendid 'Great House' on Jamaica, to which they invited us to accompany them in their chartered local ketch. This we gladly did, and spent some relaxed days in the utmost luxury, surrounded by, surprisingly, superb pictures, tapestries, furniture and other treasures from their famous Lincolnshire house, Belton. As Brownlow himself had been King Edward VIII's Lord-in-Waiting at the time of the Abdication, and had had the delicate job of conveying Mrs. Simpson away to France, he had plenty of gossip with which to entertain us. That he certainly did, with all the expertise of the born raconteur, as well as telling us story after story of his travels and adventures around the world. These were many, and his telling of them was spell-binding. I can see us yet, as in some Conrad story, complete with cigar and more tropical scents, sitting out on the terrace looking down at the moonlit sea, with Brownlow's monologue going on and on, Lady Brownlow,

[1] Peregrine, Baron Brownlow, 1899–.

Amabel and myself entranced as he spun his astonishing web of precisely chosen and melodiously spoken words. Entirely accidental and unforeseen as it was, our few days stay at that unlikely Great House near Roaring River remains unforgettable.

Lunching at Government House (all scaffolding within for the repair of ceilings brought down by a recent earth-tremor) I was plonked down at table next to Princess Alice, Chancellor of Jamaica University. She was, I was warned, dead set on the building of a chapel to complete the campus, which no-one else wanted—partly because of the Island's multiplicity of religious sects—one, 'The Carnal Baptists', about which my curiosity was never satisfied. It emerged that what the Princess really wanted was a great Gothic edifice reminiscent of Henry VII's chapel, Westminster Abbey or the St. George's Chapel at Windsor, and it was up to me, I gathered, to wean her from such extravagant imaginings. I did my best, stressing the unsuitability of such structures in a tropical climate, the impossibility of securing the materials and skills essential for their reproduction today on a Caribbean island, their incompatibility with what had already been built, all modern and functional, though with an unusual graciousness that responded perfectly to a lovely setting. Though I have no idea what, if anything, all this chapel bow-wow accomplished, the ploy was anyway aborted, and I think a badly needed physics laboratory took its intended place. Also at this luncheon was Lord Reith, an old colleague of mine as Chairman of one of the New Towns. He had just flown in from Caracas where he had clearly been deeply impressed by the Venezuelans' tremendous works in seeking to expand and glorify their capital. 'If only,' he sighed, '*We* had had that sort of money to play with!'

I have, on several occasions and to me quite inexplicably, been mistaken for somebody else—first Kenneth Barnes, director of the Royal College of Dramatic Art, then Hannen Swaffer, a prominent left-wing journalist—and I was once asked for my autograph in the belief that I was Bertrand Russell. The only time when mistaken identity was at all embarrassing was on this visit to Jamaica, which was during Bustamente's premiership. I was time and time again taken for the great man himself and cheered or booed accordingly, demonstrations that were naturally bewildering until I discovered whom I was thought to be, my deep suntan having by then approximated to his own complexion.

Fiji, on the atlas, looked a good place to make a rendezvous with both our New Zealand daughter, Dr. Charlotte Wallace, and the sun—and so it proved, much of our time there being spent in and under the lukewarm sea. We were a little startled at having our baggage searched and being ourselves actually 'frisked', though we co-operated zealously when we learnt that what was feared was the accidental importation of the dreaded Rhinoceros Beetle, whose ravages could be devastating. We learnt all we could possibly hold about the island's agricultural and other problems, advantages and history, from a young Fijian chief who, though now of no political significance, seemed to command universal respect, as his intelligence, charm and fine presence seemed fully to warrant. We were put in his able charge by the Governor, who told us that though our guide had been educated in England (and obviously very well) his much respected grandfather had of course been a cannibal. His father, however, was not, and we indeed attended some ceremonial occasion at his island court that was decorous in the extreme.

At the end of our stay, Amabel returned to New Zealand with our daughter, whilst I flew on to spend a week or so in Mexico, variously divided between pre-Columbian monuments, Jesuit Baroque churches and contemporary 'high life'; this last through a merchant banker connection, Jack Hambro, who had given me an introduction to a most hospitable international tycoon with a town house in Mexico City. He owned, as well, a very charming country retreat with a wonderful garden that inter-penetrated the courts and loggias of the house itself, so that you were never quite sure whether you were indoor or out. This seemed the entirely apt architectural response to the climate and the altitude, that together with the beauty of the countryside had attracted a number of rich Americans to the place. I was told that dollars were worth several times their home value there, so that even the not so absurdly affluent could still afford pretty grand houses and lots of servants. Not that that would have mattered to Barbara Hutton, or whatever she was currently called (the

Woolworth heiress anyway) who was, I gathered, building a house there *underground*, for no reason that I could discover other than *pour le chic*.

Being a little dazed after a succession of cocktail parties in three or four houses, each vying with the rest in exotic elegance, followed by a dinner party out on a pergolaed terrace, I asked my host 'For goodness sake, what sort of a place *is* this—I simply can't make it out'. 'Well,' he replied, 'it has been called, rather unkindly "a place in the sun for shady people".' This description seemed to have some support when it was suggested that I might care to be shown over the most sumptuous house in the whole colony by the caretaker, which could readily be arranged in the owner's absence. Being duly impressed by the splendour of the interiors I was shown, I was full of curiosity about the owner himself, obviously a man of considerable taste and knowledge. 'Oh, he's in prison' was my host's reply to my enquiry as to whether I should be meeting him, 'The usual thing you know, that isn't ordinarily discussed nor ordinarily taken official notice of, but being so very rich, he should be good for quite a big ransom and so well worth locking up until he pays it.' As a sample of the administration of justice, this was accepted with a shrug as inevitable under the existing regime. I had several times passed by the Presidential Palace, always hemmed in by a large concourse of cars, and I had remarked that the President seemed extraordinarily popular or at any rate unusually accessible, or else a non-stop party giver. 'All wrong' I was told, 'They are all guards and secret police.'

However politically uninvolved one may be, there is a certain unease in being astray without a word of Spanish in a country run by what I supposed was a corrupt dictatorship, and it was quite definitely reassuring to have a talk with our ever-so British Ambassador. At his embassy I recorded a joint broadcast with the architect of Mexico's University City who, truth to tell, I liked a good deal better than his buildings—for all their world celebrity as the then latest thing in virile modernism. Then, of all things, I was asked to record a talk on Portmeirion as (so it seemed) the place was already pretty widely known, at least amongst the considerable English colony, as indeed I discovered when invited to a sort of cabaret club where they were doing a play of Christopher Fry's, and rather well.

My intended hotel, recommended by Patrick Blackett,[1] couldn't take me in—nor could some half dozen others to which my airport taxi hopefully took me, but around midnight we did land up at one that, though obviously unfinished, had a lighted doorway and where I was told I could have a bed if I did not also expect food, hot water or service. As it happened, these deficiencies did not signify, as I was quickly rescued by another friendly contact who wanted my opinion on his proposals to develop a magically beautiful lakeside property of his, some distance away, to which he took me. There were terrific opportunities for exploiting the natural advantages of the place, to their unquestioned enhancement if the right steps were taken in the right order, but though my advice was eagerly sought and willingly given, I don't know whether it was acted on or whether my realtor (he had bought the territory to develop it anyhow) disgraced himself and it by clumsy sub-division, or did the right thing and was deservedly enriched.

Baroque-orientated as I am, I found the contorted richness of the Mexican version of the style rather too much even for me, while I was inclined to be repelled rather than attracted by most of the pre-Columbian artifacts, as indeed by Diego Rivera's harsh ideological and historical murals. So, by my own fault no doubt, I did not find Mexico as aesthetically rewarding as I had hoped, though I was active enough in my pursuit of its culture. Indeed over-active in that high altitude, for bounding up one of their steep-stepped pyramids, I more or less collapsed at its summit, to be revived by a kind American already resting there with a draught from a Coca-Cola bottle fished out from his haversack—another new experience never since repeated.

I have said that I have seldom felt embarrassed, but I had forgotten the real horror of my last half hour under my kind host's hospitable roof where, lodged in a luxurious suite, I had been valeted by a most attractive Mexican maid. I was to be driven to the distant airport in my host's Rolls, so before joining

[1] The late Lord Blackett, o.m., President of the Royal Society. Lady Blackett is still a neighbour at Brondanw.

him at breakfast, I saw that my luggage was all ready and then I remembered passport, flight tickets and my wallet, none of which could I anywhere discover. I unpacked everything, searched in every pocket or possible lurking place that I could think of—but still with no result. 'So much,' I thought, 'for "open planning"—someone has wandered in amongst the loggias and patios, entered my bedroom and left me destitute—damn!' I told my host and hostess of my predicament in an agitated speech somewhat to this effect:

'For all round embarrassment and unpleasantness, have you ever met anything to beat this? I, a perfect stranger, am wished on to you by a friend of yours in England, but you have no proof of my identity as you haven't seen my passport which I now claim is conveniently stolen, together with all my money and flight tickets. So you are stuck with me unless and until you advance me a very substantial sum of money with no sort of security on no more than your possible hunch that I am an honest man and not just a plausible rogue. On top of all, I have by implication accused your staff of laxity if not worse, and I can't even tip them as I would wish unless you lend me the money. Well, there it is and I am as sorry as can be, but what shall I do?' 'Have another really thorough search in which I will help you,' said my hostess, 'and if we still can't find the things, we will then fix you up.' And of course, to my shame and relief, she *did* find them where, as she admitted, they might very well have been overlooked.

I suggested that now I must look more thoroughly bogus than ever, cadging money on the false pretence of having been robbed! However, that possibility seems not to have been seriously entertained, as all ended in merriment and I have even got a cordial Christmas card from them every year since that awful day.

Though Indian art and architecture had never so much attracted me as had the somewhat analogous Chinese, I nonetheless agreed with Amabel that India was a country about which one should at least know something. So thither we went in the early 1960s. Landing at Bombay, we found ourselves almost at once— and I don't quite know how—seated in a marquee being addressed by Mr. Nehru in flawless English, in celebration of some anniversary of Rabindranath Tagore, supported on the platform, to our surprise and pleasure, by our old friends Leonard Elmhirst[1] and Richard Church.[2]

To see Imperial Delhi had been one of the main lures of our Indian visit so far as I was concerned. I found it a good deal less to my liking than I had hoped, if not actually a disappointment. I had studied all the plans and photographs in my great folio volumes of Lutyen's works—edited by my old assistant Andy Butler—but for one thing, I had not realized that the prevailing colour of the stone was a sort of stuffy pink and not the off-white of my imagination. Whilst except for some vast and necessarily very rare public occasion, its wide open spaces and long perspectives seemed too much to transcend the human scale and make one a little tired even to contemplate. All the detailing was, as one would expect, impeccable and apt—even within the government offices where we visited various ministers. Granted that Indian motifs had to be harmonized with high classic, no-one could have contrived the marriage with such ingenuity, tact and general success as Edwin Lutyens.

He and Sir Herbert Baker had been uneasily yoked together as joint architects and I heard something of their differences from each of them, especially about siting and layout. Lutyens took an especial dislike to Sir Herbert's great drum-like office block which he called 'Baker's Dreary-go-round' and in a magazine article of mine the editor in the caption under its photograph unfortunately attributed it to 'Sir Edwin Lutyens, P.R.A.'. The first I heard of this gaffe was on a postcard from our common friend, old Sir Charles Reilly,[3] which read: 'If you want Ned ever to speak to you again, do something quickly about that picture on page 17 in . . .' So, of course, I wrote off to apologize for the mistake, though it wasn't mine, and got back: 'Can't be helped—and I daresay Baker thinks it has damaged his reputation as much as I *know* it has damaged mine.' The cats!

The immense and intricate cave sculptures that we were taken to see were certainly impressive but I have to confess that what

[1] Founder of the Dartington Hall complex and Trust.   [2] Writer and critic.
[3] Celebrated head of Liverpool University School of Architecture.

Moira Leggat, Pirnie, Kelso, Roxburghshire

Plate 1   Temple in fibreglass at Hatton Grange, Shropshire, later repeated elsewhere

Royal Commission on Ancient and Historical Monuments in Wales and Monmouthshire

Plate 2a The author's first country house, Llangoed Castle, Breconshire, 1912 . . .

Mr. Tony Mason-Hornby

Plate 2b . . . And his last, Dalton Hall, Cumbria, 1973

I actually liked best were the eighteenth- and even early-nineteenth-century official classical buildings of the British Raj. We made long excursions by hired car to a carefully selected number of especially recommended 'sights', staying in hotels of unexpected sophistication, but shocked and depressed by the extreme poverty and squalor of most villages through which we passed, where, however, we would now and again be charmed and cheered by sight of parties of women in brilliant yet subtly shaded saris of memorable beauty. We did loyally try to admire the Taj Mahal as, poor thing, current sophisticated taste has so unkindly demoted it, but it was no use. We had to admit that there was justice in Sir Hugh Casson's caustic comment when he referred to it as 'this refugee from the mantelpiece'. But we liked the monkeys.

We travelled up country to stay with Mulk Raj Annand the writer, accurately described by Amabel's brother, John Strachey,[1] as 'a sort of one-man Indian Bloomsbury' from whom we learnt more about his country's conditions than from anyone else. On again to stay with the J.B.S. Haldanes[2] in Calcutta. He was then holding a high official scientific post there and had 'gone Indian' even in the matter of dress and food, which latter we found difficult to enjoy, or sometimes even to eat. The drive in from the airport had somewhat prepared us for the slatternly squalor and poverty that pervades so much of the teeming city itself, where every Indian problem seemed to be represented and intensified. Its troubles were explained to us by the most remarkable Governor of West Bengal when she hospitably entertained us in the fine old governor's palace, left over from British India days.

Another relic is the exceedingly pompous Victoria Memorial, a great over-dressed domed building rather reminiscent of Belfast's City Hall, of which Sir Lawrence Weaver[3] remarked to me as we quizzed it together: 'Fair drips of the drawing board, don't it?' We were shown round the remarkable zoo one evening after closing time to see the enormous nocturnal fruit bats flapping out and away from their roosting trees like rags of

[1] Labour M.P. and Minister.   [2] Professor, biologist and philosopher.
[3] Architectural Editor of *Country Life*, critic and writer.

D

tattered tarpaulin against the after-glow. Next we were shown through the temple courts of some strange religious sect in session, and then an obscure and highly exotic late-at-night street market, and much else which we should have scarcely have discovered for ourselves.

But what I did find for myself and explored most thoroughly was the old British Cemetery, a truly wonderful outdoor architectural museum of funerary monuments, mostly of extreme elegance, whether obelisks, columns, urns, altar-tombs, or little pavilions, always beautifully inscribed—the only saddening thing about it all being the general youth of those commemorated—largely in their twenties. I think there can have been no burials there for generations, for certainly I cannot recall anything to offend against the classical propriety of these miniature master-pieces of the eighteenth century. For me, this cemetery was certainly the highlight of Calcutta, if not of India—perverse and even a little macabre as that may sound.

Perhaps I was already sickening for, flying back alone (Amabel had broadcasting assignments that kept her in Bombay) I was scarcely home before I went down with some unidentified but virulent infection that apparently nearly killed me. But—as usual—it didn't, and by the time Amabel had been rushed down from London airport by a car sent up from Wales to meet her Bombay plane, the doctors were out of their flap and I was quite soon as good as new again. Not long afterwards I gave the doctors another scare with a coronary thrombosis—all my own fault through fancying myself a Hercules when I wasn't. 'Oh, one of those things,' said Bertie Russell when I told him, 'I had one forty years ago in China, and was none the worse for it.' Nor was I for mine.

6

That Sixth Sense—Dreams

The trouble with my mind, so far as it still works at all, is that it does not remember things in an orderly sequence. When I remember one building or event, others that I relate to it come to mind though perhaps separated by twenty, seventy or even eighty years. This does not make for a tidy autobiography and at times forces me to deal with topics rather than events as they happen, as for instance in the following piece on dreams.

Once, long ago, I knew a highly intelligent, cultivated and happy old lady who averred that one of the main sources of her manifest pleasure in life was her dreams, as to which she claimed total recall when awake. It was Mrs. Arnold-Forster, who I think wrote a book about her enviable 'night life'. As she also had considerable, though by no means complete, control over the plots of her dreams, is it small wonder that she valued them highly, especially as that most enjoyable dream sensation of 'flying' could apparently be hers 'on demand'. Her rare ability to fly secretly and swiftly was of course recognized by our Government as of inestimable value in time of war, and fully exploited to its (and her own) great satisfaction. My dream flying is, alas, very rare but enough to make me envious of her great good fortune.

I have my compensations. One is my ability to conjure up the most superb landscapes, generally as backdrops to some quite trivial happening in the foreground. Whatever Constable, Claude, Turner, Wilson, or Gainsborough painted, I shamelessly borrow as my backdrops, with my own impertinent alterations, omissions and additions to suit my theme, or from mere caprice. I would have expected, rather, to borrow my 'sets' from Canaletto or Palladio. But I suspect that my unconscious is aware that plagiarizing *them* would involve a lot of accurate detailing that I could not reproduce with sufficient plausibility to be convincing, whereas conjuring up sunsets, skyscapes, mountain crags, waterfalls and forest glades leaves one's own fancy relatively free to splurge about ad lib.

Though thoroughly enjoyable, I can only recall such scenic displays in a vague and 'atmospheric' way, whereas pretty silly and apparently meaningless little set pieces of drama that sometimes intrude can stick clearly in my mind long enough to be recorded in a scribbled note. For example :

Part of a Multiple Dream. Early Morning, 31 December, 1974—Written Down Before Noon That Day

It seemed to have been generally agreed that the grand new festival ball-room (rather like the Inigo Jones Banqueting House—the state re-opening of which by the Queen Mother I had attended) should be opened by *me*. I thought it a very proper proposal and promised active and cordial co-operation.

I arranged for an impressively augmented Viennese dance-band to be mounted (all in Ruritanian uniform) on banked tiers at the entrance end, facing a high gallery at the further end, from which at the opening bars of the first waltz I would leap from atop the balustrade and float gracefully down to the dancing floor with my opera cloak as parachute, and dance the length of the ballroom alone, between the applauding ranks of the other guests.

I first showed myself to the admiring audience below, balanced on the balustrade, got up as though a stage character from 'Die Fledermaus'—full evening dress, of course, opera cloak and gibus hat, white gloves and all.

I had had long debate with the bandmaster as to the most suitable music for my *pas-seul*, and having tried passages from several including 'The Choristers', 'The Chocolate Soldier', and half a dozen others, chose 'Gold and Silver' and conducted a rehearsal myself to ensure precisely the right tempo and emphasis.

That assured, I ascended to my balcony—bowed gracefully to the up-turned faces below, and then launched myself into mid-air to float quite slowly down to the dancing floor—throwing kisses right and left. Having landed and danced myself back to the band without seeking a partner (I didn't seem to know any of those present) I sat down to a little card table and started drafting a scheme for the embellishment and civilized development of an entrancing little archipelago of islands somewhere in the tropics, under the rather disapproving eyes of a grumpy old gentleman with whiskers.

But I was called suddenly away to attend to an important job I was engaged on at the time—the rationalization and better use of parts of Hampton Court Palace. The Office of Works had asked that somehow or other I should contrive a large assembly room out of a rather muddled complex of little apartments that were considered too substandard and awkward for modern usefulness. I was however also instructed to preserve anything I could of what existed.

I had in fact managed to produce a fine, well-proportioned assembly room—all finished save for final decoration, which I displayed with some pride to the high civil servant who was making an official inspection on behalf of the Ministry.

He agreed that I had given a most satisfactory answer to the problem set—but why had I left an old fashioned painted bath with claw and ball feet, and a mahogany-cased loo with a high-up chain-pull plug in one corner?

'Oh', I said. 'There wasn't anything else of any architectural or historic interest to preserve—so rather than disappoint your Minister, I have kept these.' 'Humph', he said, and vanished.

It ought to be recorded (as I reported to the Ministry) that I had received the most wonderful and unexpected assistance from a charming and endlessly resourceful little boy of about twelve who clambered like a monkey all over the place—up chimney stacks, into dark roof-spaces and along dubious beams, and shouted down to me clear and technically valuable information as to what he found. I never came across such an able, amiable and co-operative little boy, and I tried to get him a permanent job with the Ministry of Works—but they said that at twelve he was really too young to be seriously considered.

Another Dream—After Trying to Make Sense of Some 'Speechless Old Woman' Film

The curtain rises on complete darkness—the only sound a confused whispering.

Presently the cloaked figure of an elegant and smiling young woman appears and seats herself on a three-legged stool awaiting her at the left hand front corner of the stage. There are no other props save a smallish globe at the opposite front corner and, more or less central, a vaulting horse and a brass eagle lectern, suggesting that the setting is either a gymnasium or a church or both. The woman is carrying a shooting-stick and, on reaching her allotted position, plants it alongside the stool, but spike uppermost, and proceeds to sit on it. She is not actually punctured however, because the spike is really only of rubber. (The intelligent spectator realizes that this ploy is intended to indicate that, despite her serene and cheerful mien, the young lady is (basically) a confirmed masochist—a fact assumed to be important in the unfolding of the as yet obscure plot.)

She proceeds to croon, sweetly and clearly, the 'Three Blind Mice' nursery rhyme, her rendering being followed by a full volume elaborately orchestrated version of the simple tune on a thundering organ, with all possible effects. She listens startled and mystified at this mighty echo of her little song, but still more so by the rolling peal of thunder and blinding flash that follow it. She is still listening, open-mouthed, when a loud basso-profundo voice declaims:

'Woman, thou art damned.'

'Damned! Why?'

'For singing that wicked song, blaspheming the most Holy Trinity.'

'Oh, *that*. But who are you anyway?'

'I am the Holy Trinity's trusted and ever-watchful P.R.O.—a most important and valuable agent, I may say, and I can't have my position jeopardized by ignorant little chits like you. I am bound to take official notice and report.'

'But what?'

'You will know soon enough.'

The young woman walks across the front of the stage and up to the globe, which has revealed itself as a turnip lantern. As she regards it, it swells up into the nursery likeness of the moon—'The Man' very clearly defined. As she caresses his 'head' great tears well up in his eyes and trickle down his cheeks.

'Poor old moon,' she says. 'Have *you* done something naughty too?'

'Not that I know of,' he sobs, 'I only want to be just left alone—
as I always have been until now—it's really too bad, it isn't fair.'

*A dream during the Blitz in London, when I was already on the govern-
ment (Hobhouse) Committee for National Parks and plugging their
cause at meetings all over the place. I cannot recall taking it down
immediately on waking, and I suspect it of being a tidied-up version
written down some time later:*

Scene: Doctor's consulting room (Doctor and Patient discovered).

Doctor: (Finishing examination—patient doing up his shirt and
collar).

Nothing organically wrong—not yet. Nerves, yes, and so
digestion, temper, spirits, professional competence and all
the rest are affected.

Sorry—can't pretend you are an interesting case—hardly
a 'case' at all. You are just the average modern town
dweller. No, not average, because you are well enough
off to cease to be so if you want—and to pay me my
proper fee—both sadly exceptional—three guineas, thank
you.

Silly, I know, to talk of any conditions of life we make
for ourselves as being 'unnatural' but . . . (telephone rings)
. . . yes . . . yes . . . we are all ultimately animals and not
machines . . . (squeal of brakes outside above the muted roar
of the London traffic and crash and hullabaloo) and we can't
forget that with impunity (fire engines and ambulance
bells). Old Lethaby warned us about becoming 'mechanical
men in a macadamized world'. (Telephone rings) Yes,
right, A.R.P. air-raid practice 8.45 tonight—anti-aircraft
battery practice—anti-gas respirators—all right.

Well, if I hadn't a partner who took over all this for me
for a couple of months every summer, whilst I hid in the
country—I should soon be nuts myself.

Patient: You don't mean . . . ?

Doctor: My dear sir—of course not—a spell of real quiet in real
honest-to-God country every so often and you would stand
even this crazy racket—at least for some years, without
batting an eyelid. I'm not worried about *you*—but my *poor*
patients—no time off and no money to speak of. No good

recommending *them* a month's yachting in the Hebrides. How and where can I find *them* assured peace and natural loveliness within a few hours and a few shillings of their homes?

One or two of my rich friends with private parks allow a few of my proteges to camp there on my going bail for their good behaviour—but half a million families ought to do what my half-dozen are doing—not on sufferance in private parks, but as of right in *national* ones.

False Alarm (*a sort of waking dream*)

As a keen amateur sailor and for a long time skipper of my own yacht, I always relished a sea voyage of any sort— even the rather featureless crossings of the Atlantic and Pacific; but now that passenger steamers are everywhere being withdrawn in favour of jet planes—just as sailing ships were making way for steam in my youth—the actual travelling to anywhere—however swift—I regard as a tedious bore and about as adventurous as a London tube ride from Euston to Victoria.

In the earlier days of flying there was, of course, an appreciable amount of risk to keep one interested, but now, even with the chance of hi-jacking, the odds on an incident of any sort are, statistically, almost nil. But before air-travel had reached that stage, I do recall one flight that I had to take abroad just after the last war in an unconverted bomber, when I had so strong a presentiment of imminent disaster that I left a moving letter of farewell behind me.

Of course, nothing whatever happened. So much for forebodings and pre-cognition!

7

Men, Women and Buildings

It may amuse one to remember and record all the oddities and quirks of those one has worked with, and I did so to some extent in *Architect Errant* under the heading of 'A Spectrum of Clients' which I now extend a little in my attempt to explore and reveal some of the incalculable outside chances that inevitably shape an architect's day-to-day concerns but, ultimately, his whole career. Of course, the picture is as I see it though I admit that a joint symposium by a representative body of outspoken clients on the tiresomeness and merits (if any) of the architect they employed might well give a truer picture of an anyhow tricky relationship than any I myself can contrive.

An architect should never be surprised by anything, but I did wonder what it might mean when a man of whom I had only heard but never met, wrote to me suddenly out of the blue to ask if I could arrange to meet him with (mysteriously) 'a view to discussing a project that I have in mind where I think your advice would be helpful'. In due course I visited him in his large and luxurious country house Nantclwyd Hall, where I gathered

he proposed to abandon the whole elaborate set-up and settle
himself anew in a beautiful setting on a distant part of the estate
that would lend itself to spectacular landscape embellishment
and be free from all the misguided extensions, 'improvements'
and muddled clutter that his predecessors had bequeathed to
distress him.

Marvelling at so much being so lightly abandoned, I did nonetheless prepare two alternative drafts for the proposed new deal,
though pointing out that for a decade or so he would be merely
exchanging old clutter for new whilst all the building and landscaping works were completed—perhaps ten years with bulldozers still clattering around and another ten before his imagined
setting could become reality. I should have greatly enjoyed
building either (or both) of my 'alternative' houses, but I could
not smother my sympathy with the old one. For all its disfiguring
mis-handling, there still remained a charming Charles II wing on
to which great lumps of building had been grafted, with some—
but not nearly enough—attention to the parent stock. Even
worse, for some reason the whole giant complex looked due
north, whilst to the south an incoherent muddle of miscellaneous
outworks, added servants' wings, laundries, garages, workshops,
kennels and a great red-brick and cast-iron water-tower enjoyed
the sunshine. It really all looked just about as welcoming as a
railway marshalling yard. Despite all this, the already well-
timbered park offered all sorts of tempting opportunities for
landscape exploitation and granted the reverse of the house
back-to-front and the consequent internal replanning and external
building—there you were with the old house, rationalized, re-
born and once more beautiful. Despite my initial scepticism, the
project was carried out: from the 'marshalling yard', newly
created terraces and gardens, new vistas, stretch towards the
near horizon, enlivened by four temples, an obelisk and a round
tower folly; a domed doric rotunda is reflected in the lake, and a
couple of new bridges span the river which, in order not to
appear absurd beneath the grandest of these, had to be specially
widened; a railway which passed through the park, made
redundant by Beeching, served for a new driveway, entered from
the main road through a monumental triple arched gateway.

Equally grandiose are the two 'side' entrances, columns sur-mounted by eagles, all as fine as can be, and the three-storeyed clock tower arch giving entrance to the garage yard, where guests' dogs can reside in comfort in specially provided palladian kennels. Of course, there have been many other projects discussed and abandoned, including a column to challenge that in Trafalgar Square. Whenever my client visits the place (he mostly lives elsewhere) there will always be a crop of new ideas—not now so readily realized, and anyhow I have now at last told him that at my age I can no longer stand the pace of an exhilarating architectural point-to-point.

Naturally we had our differences—he never agreed to provide the tall fountain jet I wanted in one of our perspectives, and I opposed (unsuccessfully) his provision of *two* heated swimming pools as unnecessary, although admittedly one was in a glazed pavilion and the other under the sky. *And* we had differences of opinion about the optimum location of the billiard room, which has travelled to the top of the house, and down again to the bottom of it, each time with the necessary strengthening of the floor and the dismantling and reassembling of the table itself. It is now, I believe, about to leave the house altogether, option number five being considered, but without me. Of course my insatiable collaborator and client, a modern variety of the eighteenth-century noble 'builder', or a reincarnated Harun al Raschid, ought to have been an architect himself and after a dozen years or more alongside me and at less than half my age—why not? He will never be content just to sit still and see beauty achieved. He will always itch to improve it.

The designing of monuments and follies I find particularly congenial, so that a sudden request for a classical temple to give point to a chain of lakes in a beautiful Shropshire park, was a most pleasant surprise. It was to be reminiscent of one I had long ago built in Cheshire, but this new one needed to be far larger and consequently different in detail and construction. What finally went up was an elegant eight-columned, domed, Doric rotunda, the whole in reinforced glass-fibre, the components handled and erected by a mobile crane on prepared foundations. The columns and cornice were simulated Portland stone, the dome green-weathered copper, with an interior night-sky ceiling featuring signs of the Zodiac relating to my client and his wife. This adventurous little temple found such general favour that it has been several times repeated and I call it my 'Stop-me-and-buy-one' folly.

Although I will no longer take on major jobs, professing myself too old and infirm, I still declare myself always willing to design tombstones for my friends. I have now built up a reasonable collection of such monuments and memorials, most notably those for Lloyd George, one in his native Llanystymdwy, and another, prestigiously unveiled by the Prince of Wales in the presence of the Prime Minister and other party leaders, in Westminster Abbey.

A memorial column on a far-distant hilltop in Devon involved me in my latest clash with an imp which has consistently plagued me throughout my life, specializing in parting me from my luggage on skilfully chosen occasions when the loss was well calculated to cause maximum inconvenience. Some of the less upsetting occasions I have charitably forgotten, but I think the first one that rèally mattered was when, due to catch a boat train on my way abroad, with an unusually imposing pile of baggage, I dumped it all outside a telephone box whilst I made a quite unnecessary farewell call, to emerge and find all I had deposited gone clean away.

After being demobilized at the end of the Kaiser's War, I had celebrated my release by a recklessly extravagant re-fit and investment in civilian clothes, including a new Sholte dress suit, with all else on the same regardlessly lavish scale. These fine feathers obviously deserved an equally distinguished new pig-skin case, which I proudly loaded onto the back platform of our little bull-nosed Morris Oxford car, aimed at our first post-war weekend house-party—a rather grand one—away in Worcester-shire. We made it all right—but not my suitcase, which it appeared I had forgotten to strap on.

Once, en route for Scotland, my suitcase was stolen from me on the underground on my way to catch my pre-arranged train at Euston. It disappeared, for ever. Even more embarrassing was arriving at Oxford from Wales for a long-arranged ball fixture, with a special partner, without a shred of my carefully selected finery. I had in fact come on from another ball that had run merrily on nearly all night and left me many hours short of sleep. So, having stacked my traps neatly on one seat of an empty compartment, I lay gratefully down on the other to catch up on my sleeping, well knowing that I should inevitably be woken up at Oxford, my destination, by the noisy invasion of that particularly popular train.

We reached Oxford. In poured the London-bound Oxonians, but where was my luggage? It had vanished without trace, evidently quietly whisked away by some stealthy intruder, whilst I peacefully slept. So there I was, punctually arrived, but destitute of all my carefully checked ballroom finery and too late to buy, hire or borrow make-shift substitutes. My promised partner refused to go on without me, so our carefully planned night out together dwindled to a rather wistful little dinner a deux—a just possible romance nipped cruelly in the bud.

Though my plaguey imp seems to have a rather primitive luggage fixation, it by no means lacks ingenuity and even some sense of malicious fun. For this latest jape (and I hope its last, as it surely deserves to be) it had the nerve to involve no less a dignitary than Dr. Ramsey, the Archbishop of Canterbury. We were both involved in the dedication of the above-mentioned memorial monument. For both of us a long and inconvenient journey seemed to be involved. Then a privately chartered jet plane was miraculously laid on, which picked me up at an R.A.F. airfield only ten miles away from my Snowdonian home, the Archbishop being already aboard. The deeply impressive ceremony over, I was duly dropped off at the same nearby airfield, while His Grace flew on to London, all according to plan.

Arrived home I immediately and prudently opened up my suitcase so as to have my muddy gumboots and wet overcoat and so on dried out and cleaned. But what met my astonished gaze was not the squalid heap of my sopping cast-offs, but the prestigious canonicals of the Primate, neatly folded. I foresaw possible Sunday complications if the vestments were still missing, so I telephoned Lambeth Palace at once. 'I'm sorry, Sir, but His Grace has already left for Canterbury,' was his secretary's response;

'I will pass on your message.' I said, 'Please tell him I will send back his things by road, first thing tomorrow.' Which I did, to Lambeth Palace, by a car from Portmeirion conveniently returning to London. My accompanying letter of apology was most handsomely acknowledged with the assurance that the swap had not, in fact, mattered and the hope that my own lost property would rejoin me as swiftly as had his. In fact it did, in the same car that had restored his to him, so that my imp's mischievous intervention actually caused the very minimum of trouble.

Still, my hope is that it may be its last fling—either because it was a relative flop as a trouble-maker, or because the involvement of the Primate of All England in its machinations would be considered a daring exploit to end on. In my own defence I would like to say that Archbishops should not go about with precisely the same humble reach-me-down blue fibre suitcases fitting enough for the common citizen—and me. Surely something saddler-made in pig-skin, bearing an engraved mitre would seem to be called for!

I was just announcing my own long-delayed retirement from actual architectural practice, because of my absurd age, when an unforeseen obstacle loomed up suddenly in my path. It took the shape of a spirited but perplexed young couple (of whom I was only distantly aware) who had inherited an extensive and romantically lovely estate in Cumbria, called Dalton Hall, some hundreds of miles away from my own habitat. But there was a horrid fly in their otherwise so welcome ointment, in the shape of a monstrously overgrown and incoherent mansion that could only have been comfortable but never convenient, even with a domestic staff well into double figures, and that neither employer nor employed would willingly even attempt to run today, at whatever cost or whatever the wages. They had the idea that this was the sort of puzzle that I had often dealt with elsewhere, and anyway, would I please advise them how best to cope with their teasing problem.

Though amply old enough to be the grandfather of both of them, and therefore great-grandfather of their entrancing young family I could not resist the challenge—nor tried to—as I foresaw nothing but harmonious co-operation, come what might. The obvious first step was an actual and thorough inspection, so away I was whisked to make just that, and report.

The commanding site was indeed well chosen, but the house itself (to me at least) an architectural nightmare. Not because of any vulgarity, there was none of that, but because of ill-considered successive extensions and botchings that failed to make either logical, functional or workable sense or achieve any sort of architectural unity. It just didn't 'add up', yet evidence remained that at some time an architect *had* been around—most notably in a quite scholarly dark Doric *porte-cochere* that rather forbiddingly, welcomed you to enter a vast glass-domed staircase atrium through an intervening vestibule whence onwards through a succession of great bleak reception rooms or, turning leftwards, into a bewildering labyrinth of dank service quarters. But the most memorable exhibits were the large areas of virulent and obviously active dry-rot, well established in the roof and the upper floors.

To deal effectively with well-established dry-rot is at best a teasing job, and can be hideously costly, and then when all is done, however thoroughly, there remains a haunting fear that some-where, something may have been missed and that the dreaded thing may yet declare itself afresh and necessitate further harassing and expensive operations. Anyway, it was the dry-rot that was finally decisive. Without it, one might have wasted a lot of time in an attempt to reduce and re-organize the status quo into present-day sense and workability and even architectural respect-ability, but only at an unforeseeable and anyhow unjustifiable cost. Merely to cope with the existing dry-rot menace would cost many unrewarding thousands, after which you would have saved what? An ungainly white elephant, unwanted by anyone.

With a clear conscience, I unequivocally recommended the total demolition and a fresh start, on the self-same well-chosen site. This was agreed between us as the right course, and whilst the cranes and bulldozers were clearing the site, I sketched out draft plans and elevations of what I thought would best suit the life-style of my young friends and their family, be worthy of its lovely setting and, incidentally, please *me*. Nonetheless, this did not prevent local patriots, whose urge for conservation was overmastering, from bitterly reproaching my client for daring to do away with the incubus. But it is heartening to find public interest in these matters aroused at all, so that one must be tolerant of occasionally mistaken zeal.

Seldom can architect and clients have been so like-minded or closely co-operative. My draft was accepted at once with acclaim and—when fully detailed and only slightly modified here and there after all three of us had gone closely into the practical effect of any minor changes—begun. The same unanimity extended to the forecourt and gardens layout and the design and placing of their several embellishments, and we have not yet decided which of the three of us is most pleased with the final result of our so co-operative effort.

I had prudently made conditions as to my part in the affair. I must be fetched and returned whenever I was needed on the site. A really reliable and qualified local site architect must be engaged to control the actual execution of the work, and moreover a first-rate general contractor found with a staff of properly skilled and experienced craftsmen. I never had such pre-conditions better met, and from clients down to the boy who cleaned the buckets and made the tea, all was eager friendliness. I can only recall one single instance of dismay and near recrimination when, Oh Horror! it was found that the drawing-room fire simply would *not* draw, but filled the place with dense wood-smoke. Whatever *could* have gone wrong, for fireplaces and flues have ever been one of my minor pet concerns. It emerged in the end that it was neither my fault nor the builders' but a mis-chance in a million. A sheet of brown paper from the fire's first lighting had been carried straight up the chimney (so good the draught!) and had been pressed and firmly lodged against the copper bars built into the chimney top to prevent birds nests blocking the flues— as *we* had now done for ourselves!

All concerned are, I think, equally pleased with the final result of our joint efforts—a moderate sized house, symmetrical on all four elevations, with classical pilastered pediments front and back. Done again, I would fatten it a trifle, so as to allow of a more generous main staircase—shallower steps and a half-landing, but its users have never complained and anyhow, there is a

Plate 3*b* Nantclwyd Hall, the new south front

Mr. Tony Mason-Hornby

Plate 3*a* The author, at the age of ninety, inspecting the roof
timbers at Dalton Hall

Plate 4a   Nantclwyd Hall, bridge carrying the new drive

Plate 4b   The re-modelled village street at Cornwell, Oxfordshire

perfectly good lift! It is very warming to have ended my long building career with so satisfying a last fling, and to find that I was still effectively operational—even to the extent of climbing ladders quite confidently!

As one grows old, one accepts the gradual thinning out of one's friends through death as being both natural and inevitable, but I had *not* been prepared to find myself out-living a number of my own architectural off-spring. In London one must, alas, expect assault and battery at any moment, but outside, in open country, I had comfortably assumed that an apt and substantial building would survive, on its own merits. But I had reckoned without appreciating the full impact of the speculative developer who, taking advantage of shifting economic conditions, is apparently prepared to demolish just anything whatsoever if he smells a profit in its replacement.

This rapacious destruction is now at least curbed where 'listed' buildings are concerned, and some of mine have been so saved, though the destruction of one at least was actually hastened by the speculator getting wind of the Government's *intention* to schedule it—and so rushed in his bulldozers ahead of the embargo. Thus far I know of four of my especially cherished buildings that have perished. Three country houses and one country restaurant— the three simply to clear the site for profitable bungalow develop- ment—the restaurant, at Laughing Water in Kent, more legitimately, to make way for a larger and grander replacement that its success over a generation had called for.

I have long been especially concerned over two of my architec- tural children—one the memorial hall for Bishop Stortford College that had been defaced by the unthinking removal of the urns that crowned its pilastered facade on the score of easier maintenance, *before* it was protected from such mutilation by official scheduling. It was in fact the first by a living architect to be so protected. The responsible authority quite failed to understand my consternation and only reluctantly agreed to the status quo being restored if it were done at my own expense and not theirs! Now, at long last, this slighting has been rectified.

But what has loomed most saddeningly for a year or two past has been the threat of total demolition of my first major job,

E

Llangoed Castle. In the spacious days of 1912 I received my first really important commission, which was to plan and get built a 'Capital Mansion House' for a large and very beautiful estate on the banks of the River Wye in Breconshire—to replace the half-ruined remnants of a seventeenth-century house that had itself replaced the original mediaeval castle.

The setting was everything one could possibly desire, the great river flowing past, a grove of fine old cedars, the hanging wood of beech and oak that sheltered the level meadows. Add to all that a client eager to grace the site with a large and gracious house answerable to all its happy surroundings and to his own ideas of 'gracious living'. He had the means to satisfy these ideas and a considerable feeling for architecture, and he agreed with my first outline proposals almost at once and author-ized the preparation of fully detailed working drawings, from which the actual house very soon began to rise. The sudden out-break of the 1914 War quickly removed architect, client and contractor to other spheres of usefulness, but found the house near enough completed to serve as a hospital, lacking only certain more or less decorative finishes—the panelling of the galleries, pilasters and cornices in the dining-room and such like.

At the war's end all, or nearly all, these deficiencies were made good and the great house settled down to mellow and be absorbed into its welcoming garden setting. When my client died, and then at a great age his widow, there was no direct heir and the inheritor's means were not such as to enable him to live in the sort of style for which the house was planned. So, although he still wished to live on the same spot, which is central to the estate and close to the home farm which he runs himself, he only wants quite a small house, and to make way for it sought official approval for the demolition of what I had built for his predecessor, and for very different times.

With two long galleries, half a dozen large reception rooms, some twenty bedrooms and generous service quarters to match, not to mention a monumental stable block, laundry, power-house and all the other appurtenances of a self-supporting estab-lishment, I have to admit that it has certainly outlived whatever 'fitness for purpose' it may once have possessed, in common with a host of other buildings, both secular and other, that are none-theless rightly preserved as silent witnesses to our historic past.

As the building is listed by the Department of the Environment as of Historic and Architectural Interest, it cannot be altered, still less destroyed, without the Department's permission. The owner sought such permission and a formal Inquiry was held at Brecon before a Government Inspector, where the representa-tions of those backing the application and those opposing it were heard at full length. The Inspector duly reported in detail to the Minister after the conclusion of the hearing (January 1975) and the Minister issued his decision in the following October, during which long interval I was naturally deeply anxious as to what the fate of my first major architectural work—my first-born—might be.

I have every sympathy with the present owner in what is indeed a cruel dilemma, but I naturally enough hoped that the Minister concerned would be on *MY* side and that of conservation. To ensure that, some use needs to be found for the building—preferably one that will allow at least some measure of public access, if only to certain parts at certain times. The difficulty is of successful match-making between institutions seeking habitats, and buildings awaiting socially useful tenants. There would seem to be here a role for some sort of 'National Fabrics Marriage Bureau'.

But at long last all is well—from my own point of view and that of the Castle—for the Minister has come down unequivocally on our side and firmly refused to allow the threatened demolition. One quote from his summing up will suffice to indicate his general attitude:

I am directed by the Secretary of State to say that he has considered the report of his Inspector . . . that Llangoed Castle is a very fine example of large-scale domestic architecture of its period, worthy of statutory listing in its own right, quite apart from its association with Sir Clough Williams-Ellis, its architect. Not only does the house contain a wealth of architectural detailing executed to a high standard, but its loss would be irreplaceable in quality . . ... He con-cludes that the house forms such a valuable part of our architectural heritage that there needs to be more exploration into the possibilities of its preservation. . . .

As to the embarrassed owner, our relationship throughout the controversy remained entirely civilized, though necessarily somewhat strained, but I hope that as the loser in our conflict, he will not hesitate to call on me for any help I can possibly give in the way of supplying original plans or drawings (now and long since in the safe keeping of the archivist of the Royal Institute of British Architects) or advice of any sort that could contribute towards the conservation obligations now officially imposed.

I have to recognize that I have only suffered grief at these architectural bereavements because I myself happen to have lived so unfairly long, though they do indeed distress me as do all other such casualties as evidence of the prevailing urge to destroy —recklessly. I flatter myself that my concern is general and not merely personal, and that I should not care a rap if only I could be persuaded that what had seemed good to me was being replaced by something even better, and that I could then gracefully accept the change without regrets. After all, the architectural coin, like all others, has its two sides, the delight of designing and actual building on one, the almost inevitable prospect of ultimate neglect and decay sooner or later on the other. The creations of most writers and painters bloom and then wilt and die far more quickly and completely, and if and when replaced by better, they too should have no complaint. But in all cases the operative word is 'IF'. Now and again one may have the chance of doing something towards reviving interest in some work of excellence, be it a building, a book, landscape, townscape or even a person.

8

A Peek at America

I flew on from Mexico to New York to stay with an old Rhodes Scholar friend, Joseph Brewer, Librarian to Queens University, to find myself invited with him to a party at the J. P. Morgan Library, where Lord Crawford[1] was to deliver an address. We had last met at Portmeirion, but he was over, I gathered, to bless the Americans' acquisition of a large part of his father's famous library so that, as he said, he felt very much at home still surrounded by the familiar books of his youth. The only drawback to an otherwise enjoyable evening was that the invitation implied 'black ties'—which meant a visit to the New York equivalent of Moss Bros. in search of a dinner-jacket suit, my possession of which would, I remembered, also please the dear old Cunard by which I had booked my passage home and that still liked its passengers to dress for dinner.

I looked up a now venerable architect friend, Billy Delano, with whom we had stayed on Long Island on a long ago visit. There he had showed us over some of the great chateaux and

[1] Earl of Crawford and Balcarres 1900–75.

palaces that he had built for millionaire clients—each a brilliant *tour de force* of its kind, whilst his Knickerbocker Club, of which he had made me an honorary member, would have looked entirely at home in St. James's Street, which indeed it would have vastly become. The very antithesis of a Modernist, he seemed in his gentle way the nearest equivalent in America of our own Edwin Lutyens. Next, to another old friend, Lewis Mumford, in his far away little country cottage which, with its weather-boarded walls, looked a bit frail and chilly, surrounded as it was on my visit by deep snow. However, as it was lined throughout by books, his own and others, it was in fact well insulated against the cold and indeed extremely cosy.

On yet again by Greyhound Coach to Williamsburg, which delighted me in defiance of all the moderns who deride it as a bogus, sentimental and retrograde reconstruction of no possible present-day relevance. But I just don't care! To begin with there are quite a number of distinguished original buildings still surviving and the actual plans and details of others that had vanished, together with exact maps of the whole eighteenth-century layout and full and precise inventories of what many of the houses had contained. Scholarly research, sympathetic architectural expertise and Rockefeller millions have together rescued and re-created a brilliantly convincing and entirely charming exemplar of Georgian–Colonial living conditions at their elegant best. Of course, there was the squalid reverse to this shining coin—too well known to need stressing in this little town dedicated to all that was gracious in an age that could still teach modern America many lessons that it seems to me it badly needs to learn—especially in town-planning.

On my homeward-bound Cunarder, Sir Alan Herbert[1] was one of the few passengers that I knew, insisting on a table of his own so that he could read himself across the Atlantic during meals, which he said was an anti-social practice not allowed at home. Otherwise he was, as usual, the centre of various social occasions, especially an absurd cabaret for which he wrote a typically A.P.H. nautical ballad that he sang, got up in a marvellously unlikely fancy dress to the company's delight. Touching at

[1] M.P., novelist, dramatist and wit.

Halifax and running ashore for a quick sniff at Canada, (my only one and in the dark at that, with snow falling) I returned to find Boyd Neel come aboard for a drink with A.P.H. Joining them, Alan proceeded to sell me and Portmeirion to him so persuasively that he did in fact later appear and re-appear, to the great enhancement of Portmeirion's musicality.

Somehow I have found myself at Los Angeles twice—first because my route to somewhere else involved a stop-off there, when I had only a sniff at the fabulous Hollywood set-up, second when I had to plunge head first into the extraordinary movie world in connection with a Disney film on Wales. It was very far indeed from being a congenial place to me, even in its still booming days when seemingly extreme vitality lent it a kind of magic. But I should imagine that such a place on its uppers (if that *is* its present state, I don't know) must be about the most depressing place on earth, at any rate for normally hopeful people like myself. But it clearly has its rewarding side for better informed and less fleeting visitors than myself.

My taxi-driver bringing me out from Hollywood into Los Angeles pointed out a cemetery that he said had given Waugh his ideas for (was it?) 'Whispering Glades' in his book *The Loved One*, and he even claimed to have driven him. Then he asked me, 'But why was he given a girl's name?' I told him that Evelyn was an old and honoured English surname and that my own brother-in-law bore it—John Evelyn Strachey. 'What,' he exclaimed, 'your brother-in-law! Why, I have read every book of his he ever wrote—a great man.' And he proceeded to reel off a string of titles—quite correctly. 'That turning there,' he went on, 'leads to Mr. Aldous Huxley's house—sad about his eye-sight. I drive him sometimes. You know him too, perhaps?' 'Yes,' I said, 'I used to.' Which started him reeling off a string of distinguished names in literature, philosophy and politics, his anxiety seeming to be assured that his book heroes actually existed as flesh and blood persons, even as he did. On parting from my know-all taxi man, I said. 'It seems scarcely possible that you should have chanced to drive all these people, yet you seem to know quite a lot about them—how come?' 'Well,' he replied, 'after all, I have got degrees in history, literature and philosophy, and I like to keep up with things.' He was manifestly miles above my head and I bade him a respectful good-night before my ignorance should become too disappointingly apparent.

Returning to my hotel on my last evening, I found a note from David Niven inviting me to a Beverley Hills party that same night, whether in his own or someone else's house I never discovered. But as a social experience it was all I hoped for and expected—a tight-packed collection of glittering stars, starlets, scriptwriters, directors and the rest, exchanging quick-fire shop gossip and banter right out of my own hum-drum world and far above my puzzled head. I was presently introduced to a young actress who opened with 'May be you know my grandfather, Frank Lloyd Wright?' When I said Yes, and how wonderful he was for 88, she responded with 'Well, he's actually over ninety but doesn't let on in case it might prejudice his professional architectural practice'—a typically Hollywood reaction!

When prudently groping my way through the maze of dark shrubberies to find the gate by which I had arrived, before being too far overcome by the apparently non-stop hospitality still in full swing—I collided with an entirely appropriate person also seeking escape—an exceedingly beautiful young actress. We continued our groping most companionably together and at last, emerging on to the high road, she said, 'On a night like this the lights of Hollywood look marvellous from high up on the hills— if you don't mind being seen with me in my rather vulgar raspberry coloured convertible—might you care to come?' I said I would, and how right I was, and how right she too about the view and, as it seemed to me then, about everything else—her job—its possibilities and pitfalls, its temptations and rewards, the whole strange world of the movie industry, and indeed about life in general. We paid untimely calls on one or two mutual friends including the Charles Laughtons, and then in the small hours she drove me back to my hotel.

With this most encouraging random sample accidentally dropped into my lap, so to say, my last Hollywood contact before escaping—my memories of that incredible place are definitely kindlier than else they would have been.

9

Food, Lovely Food

Having tried hard (though vainly I fear) to restrict the contents of this tiresomely jerky book to matters of possible general interest, and to confess my own usually minority views—I feel it only honest that I should at last reveal my private intermittent interest in food—not in the least obsessive, but there nonetheless, as it were, 'on call' as and when the occasion may suggest. With all manner of things of admittedly greater importance long forgotten, how is it that a whole series of related but trivial events should still be vividly recalled despite my notoriously bad memory?

I am not a greedy man, in fact I have a singularly small appetite, nor am I a true gourmet as even the most recherché dishes can often leave me quite unmoved. Yet, for some eighty years back I still retain vivid recollections of eating something, the deliciousness of which became, on the instant, forever unforgettable. Having long puzzled over this odd quirk of mine in the hope of finding some rational explanation, I have been driven, for want of a better, to the perhaps untenable hypothesis that through some peculiar disarrangement of nerves, or electro-microcircuits, there

must be some sort of hit-or-miss 'hot line' from my taste buds
to the most retentive memory section of my brain that may just
happen to operate, or may not. The earliest manifestation of this
curiously erratic selectivity was when I was only eight and
encountered a seemingly perfect brawn at home in Caernarvonshire—soft, grey, gelatinous and peppery, and it has remained my
Platonic model for all brawns ever since. Next in time was a
sandwich eaten in a pub at Eynsham in Oxfordshire, where
superb fatty smoked ham smeared with mustard lay between
crusty slices of well buttered fresh home baked bread. Simple
tastes? Well, yes, to some extent, though my next exhibit is a
perfectly cooked fat little hen quail sitting on its soft pad of
gravy-sodden toast, eaten at a ball-supper at the Ritz. It may well
be that my supper partner had something to do with the sharpened
activity of my hypothetical 'hot line', but all the quail I have
ever encountered, before or since, have unfairly to compete with
that one, still unsuccessfully.

The four years of the First World War that I spent in Flanders
and France were, of course, gastronomically barren save for one
still irradiated night when one of my Welsh Guards brother
officers gave a little dinner in his rest billet behind the lines,
cooked by his most worshipful hostess who was clearly a Cordon
Bleu *manqué*. The highlight of the feast was a superb chicken
vol-au-vent—its upstanding fluted pastry jacket with a blue
riband (very appropriately) tied about its middle. My home-
coming was marked by another culinary highlight, when my
wife and I were bidden to dine with my brigadier at Claridges,
where a partridge to end all partridges has remained a lovely
memory to this day.

Next I think, it was the baked fresh-water fish that I encountered whilst being driven home convalescent by my wife,
from a visit to Austria where I had very nearly died of pneu-
monia. It was at a highly picturesque little fortified town on an
island in the middle of a lake approached by a causeway—clearly
German because a battalion of surprisingly scruffy and ill-equipped
Wehrmacht infantry with antique horse-drawn transport was
halted on its main street—but I can't remember its name or
discover it on even the largest scale map. Anyhow, I should

probably never meet the like of that fabulous fish again, even were I to return in that hope. Maybe it was indeed and in fact *partly* fabulous—its very excellence a subjective assessment by a suspect witness not long recovered from a week's delirium.

Then there were those incomparable long-ago pork pies bought from a wayside shop in Atherstone and later eaten from their paper bag as 'elevenses' by myself and family on our passage from London to Wales. Still warm and juicy from the oven, I have never again met their peers and, recognizing utter perfection when I met it, I nearly turned back for a refill, though then a dozen miles or so beyond their hallowed birth-place. Another 'elevenses' miracle later occurred, less un-expectedly, in Banbury where, perhaps in competitive emulation of its famous 'cake' for which I have no liking, the local dough-nut excelled all other such in the whole Kingdom—at any rate at that particular hour on that particular morning. Still warm, soft, light and spongy—it had a generous filling of really good rasp-berry jam—and not the mere smear of anonymous, over-boiled household' stuff too often met with that can be positively nasty.

I have always been an addict (largely deprived) of really well boiled oatmeal porridge, eaten with salt and ice-cold creamy milk, but of all things it was a T.V. programme that introduced me to the proper thing. My old friend Alistair Sim who, acting the part of a Scottish compositor or such in a film about a news-paper, was shown having supper at home and eating his porridge from two bowls—one obviously containing the stuff steaming hot, and the other cold milk into which he dipped his half full porridge spoon, all—as the captions of wartime pictures of Lord Woolton the Food Minister, tasting and recommending some dreary ersatz dish used to reiterate—'with evident relish'. Those were certainly the days for real appreciation, for un-inhibited and instant salivation at the mere whiff of a rare kipper or a bacon rasher about to grace one's breakfast.

But I am also thoroughly appreciative of higher things—roast sirloin, rare and fat, cut very thin, preferably cold, with creamy mashed potatoes—for which I look to my club, Simpsons, or Portmeirion. At home roast saddle of Welsh mutton, nettle soup and a sweet consisting of pineapple slabs supporting Swiss cheese and whipped cream, covered with ground coffee, come high in my estimation. But to end prestigiously, I still vividly recall —of all things—a green *savoury* ice, as the grand finale of a memorable luncheon in Kensington Square some time between the wars, contrived by our hostess, Ruth Welinski, widely and rightly revered as herself an inspired cook and author of *Lovely Food* and its sequel *More Lovely Food*. But I don't think she ever revealed the secret of that strange but delicious ice, certainly not to *me*. Could she have extracted the essence of caviar and/or smoked salmon, and even if so, how *green*?

Being no Arnold Bennett and so rarely a diner at his lusher 'Imperial Palace' or 'Grand Babylon' hotels, I am generally happily surprised to find how truly excellent their cooking can sometimes be, and surely should be at the prices charged. These I merely note with raised eyebrow but without dismay, as at such high-life feasting I am consistently a guest and almost never the host. Set 'banquets' very seldom live up to their menus and are generally as little memorable gastronomically as the accompanying speeches intellectually or entertainingly. Yet my latest most happy memory is of a flawless Timbale De Sole Thermidore served at a large banquet at the Dorchester given by the President of the Royal Society, Lord Blackett, to celebrate the tri-centenary of its foundation. But there again the brilliant assembly, the predictably admirable speeches, and the very occasion itself would no doubt have added reflected lustre to even the humblest of fish, plain fried—with chips.

Finally, a wistful backward glance at a lost love—or possibly one that never really existed. My favourite food, at any rate in theory, is undoubtedly *lobster*—but in actual fact it seldom, if ever, quite comes up to my high hopes and expectations. I think at *sometime* I must have met it in what to me was its full and ultimate perfection, but so long ago that I am a poor and hesitating witness as to its treatment. I *seem* to have happy memories of burnt mustard and mayonnaise, of brandy, of juicily impregnated bread-crumbs or rice, possibly a whiff of garlic. I know there are classical recipes with their appropriate names, and now and again I hopefully have another try at recapturing my long-lost rapture, but thus far in vain. A cold lobster I merely regard as a poor fish that has tragically missed its ordained and proper destiny.

And now a lament for the vanished muffin. In that great play *Man and Superman*, there is this exchange:

Tanner: At the end of the week you will find no more inspiration in her than in a plate of muffins.

Octavius: You think I shall tire of her.

Tanner: Not at all; you don't get tired of muffins. But you don't find inspiration in them.

When Bernard Shaw wrote that too-grudging tribute just seventy years ago, muffins were muffins indeed, as I can personally testify, and were universally known as something undeniably good and would have been accepted at the time as an apt symbol of quiet enjoyment and content, which I take to be his implication. But if for some reason inspiration of any sort were to visit me at all, it would be more likely to arrive along with a muffin than through any other medium. And now, one of the few sadnesses of my old age is that I shall have to live it out without the companionship and solace of those muffins that to me, at least, were my main addiction and stimuli to fruitful thought. Why are we now so cruelly deprived of this fine flower of what is yet held to be a period of advancing civilization?

My first and still poignantly-remembered encounter with the dear departed was when but half-way through a perfect example at the United Services Club I was firmly ejected by some heartless official because small boys were very strictly *persona non grata* in that prestigious institution—a fact that my kindly host had forgotten. When, in due course, I joined the club of my own, I found to my joy that its muffins, too, were superb and moreover treated with the reverence they deserved. They would come in their heated covered silver dish along with salt cellar, china tea, cream and folded napkin, and be set down at my elbow by a club waiter still in the livery of the Regency, knee-breeches, silk stockings and buckled shoes, though no longer with powdered hair, and all for no more than a shilling.

The muffins of those days, at their proper best, measured some three and a half inches in diameter and were about an inch thick and had a pallid floury skin with a sponge-like interior. After baking or toasting till they flushed a light brown, with perhaps burnt patches here and there—they were split in two, both halves being super-saturated with melted butter. And even between the two World Wars, muffins capable of such glorious transformation were still being hawked in the streets of London—at any rate on Sunday afternoons—when a man tinkling a little bell would walk slowly past our house in South Eaton Place with a tray upon his head, covered with green baize—'Muffins! Muffins!' No more, alas! But why? Ah me !

In any gastronomic one-upmanship contest, I think two of my entries should be these. First, a luncheon at La Maison Basque tête-à-tête with André Simon, founder-president of the wine and food society, and Marcel Boulestin the famous restaurateur whose first establishment in Leicester Square I contrived for him. Then dinner with Mr. Berry, the St. James's Street wine merchant, at Prunier's 'To meet seven distinguished burgundies'—an occasion which I gathered Madame Prunier had flown specially over from Paris personally to superintend. I was a little mystified by such flattering attention until I realized that, having just become a licensed victualler myself (at Portmeirion) I would have a certain patronage to bestow and might therefore be thought worth a little attention—and education.

For sheer gastronomic horror, I doubt if the breakfast coffee once served on a friend's yacht could even be matched, far less beaten. A coffee pot had been used all right, but alas! the one from which the navigation and other lamps were daily filled with paraffin. As an emetic the recipe merits the very widest publicity.

While on the subject of food, I feel justified in the following digression: A teasing legend arose, in support of my confessed weakness for opulent display and latent snobbism, that no dinner, however Lucullan, could really be quite up to my exacting standard unless served from and eaten off GOLD PLATE. It all began with my astonished report of an unlikely banquet so served at the Soviet Union's Foreign Office in Moscow. My next golden occasion was quite appropriately at the Goldsmiths' Hall in London, where I was bidden to dinner with a young prince, whom I happened to meet abroad and had got together with over architecture.

Just after the last war, I dined with Mr. Butlin (along with Jane Clark, Lord Clark's[1] wife) whom we were endeavouring to civilize to the extent of introducing a little culture into his holiday camps' so variegated diversions. Why not, we said, occasional exhibitions of good modern painting and an exposure now and again to concerts of really first rate music, classical for choice, but anyway something a bit above the usual popular ration. The dinner was all it could be from its initial caviar onwards, but though our host did make a few faltering gestures along the lines we suggested, I'm afraid our well-intentioned little ploy failed to win even a toe-hold in the day-long 'fun and games' camp programmes. In retrospect, the gold plates we had feasted off rather lost their glitter.

My last (and probably final) golden occasion was appropriately farcical and most enjoyable. I had some now-forgotten professional job or other to see to in Anglesey near to the little old Welsh Plas belonging to Lord Boston,[2] to which he sometimes retired. He heard of my fixture and said 'Though I shall be alone, do use me as your base'—and I did. I found that 'alone' was quite literally true—and a most agreeable experience. After he had served and cleared away tea, he told me what he would be cooking for dinner if I approved, and then added 'By the way, I gather that you rather like eating off gold plate. Some of mine happens to be right here, so why don't we, if you don't mind washing up afterwards whilst I see to the other chores?' It was all so madly unexpected and unlikely that I can still recall that jolly little banquet more clearly than many far more prestigious feasts.

A most agreeable and absurd finale to an anyway absurd legend.

[1] Art Historian, author of *Civilisation*.
[2] Son of first President of Council for the Protection of Rural Wales.

10

Vainglory

I am made constantly aware, in this my 95th year, of the really quite enormous changes in manners, fashions and general style of living that have taken place during my lifetime; when I see on television plans for nuclear power stations and solar generators in space, I remember that as a boy I was taken by my father to a farm where the sole source of energy for turning the butter churn was a wheel turned by a very jolly little dog, considered the very latest thing and the only source of light, strings dipped in tallow.

I must confess to a certain nostalgia for the ways of my youth, 'period pieces' though they may be. As a small boy I had the rare privilege of possessing a precious old great-aunt still surviving from Georgian times, whom we used to visit on occasions, and I dare say I seem as rare and antique to the young of today as she did to us. One of her many attractions was the possession of a wondrous album that she and her sisters had long ago embellished with famous and heroic figures, all splendidly apparelled in snippets of real silk, satin, wash-leather, velvet, tin-foil or whatever. Armour, swords, and helmets flashed, plumes of real feather (almost) waved, torches flared, and all the poses were historically appropriate, regal, menacing or declamatory as the character and the occasion seemed to demand. No doubt my several great-aunts had only to stick on to Pollocks' pre-printed outline all the trimmings that their fancy might dictate, or that were actually provided by Pollocks, along, presumably, with ready colour-printed faces. Anyway, I found this assemblage of historic or legendary notables quite intoxicating—Richard Coeur-de-Lion, Othello, Macbeth, Julius Caesar, Bonnie Prince Charlie or whoever, and compared our drab contemporary selves and the citizens of Bangor most unfavourably with these gorgeously arrayed personages of the past.

Whatever had happened to turn us all into dreary black beetles? Was this depressing blight universal or only endemic in North Wales? If some day I somehow got to London, or even abroad, might I still find the colour, gaiety and display that so entranced me? My great-aunt feared that Victorian London would disappoint me, but added that if I travelled far enough I might yet see at least outlandish and colourful traditional costumes.

I was sad that my lot had been cast in nineteenth-century, rigidly nonconformist Caernarvonshire, where *best* invariably meant *black*, instead of in, say, seventeenth- or eighteenth-century Venice, where of course I would have had my father a decadent magnifico with gorgeous mistresses attended by little blackamoor pages, dressed up in scarlet and gold. He would have a beflagged great gondola or barge, letting off fireworks, masked balls under blazing chandeliers in his palace. . . . All of which would, of course, have been utter hell to my actual grey-clad, studious father, or for that matter to most of my more recent ancestors, who had tended to be academics, squarsons or even Quakers.

I long ago confessed my secret lust for display and splendour, for the spectacular, my interest in ancient lineage and resounding historic territorial titles from such as 'His Serene Transparency' to 'The Akond of Swat'. My acute awareness of, and interest in, snobbery must I think at least suggest a like weakness in myself— a crypto-snobbery if you like—part, I suspect, of my appetite for anything 'decorative' and my out-dated but still latent conserva-

F

tism. Yet I remember that when it was patiently explained to me that someone, somewhere, had to pay for all the pomp and pleasures of my glittering nobles, I gravely pondered the matter, admitted its general truth, and then countered with, approximately, 'If I were a poor peasant with barely enough to live on or to support my family, I would still most certainly and willingly give *something* towards the support of any grandee living in splendour and thoroughly enjoying it himself. I should of course like to see some of that splendour and enjoyment, if he ever happened to pass my way, or I his, but merely to know that *someone*, somewhere, was living a colourful, gay and carefree life, would be return enough for my twopenny halfpenny subscription.'

Having this antiquarian and perverse streak, I confess to a sneaking regard for highly exclusive institutions such as The Royal Yacht Squadron, The Jockey Club, The Knights of the Garter, and even the Brigade of Guards. For all their hierarchical pretentions, privilege, and assumption of superiority, the host of small traditional observances which are mostly curious rather than tiresome, I think I see them as some sort of bulwark against some types of contemporary modernism, in manners, speech and dress, which I find slovenly and hard to admire.

I did not see much of grand club interiors until I joined the Union, then housed in a beautiful building at the corner of Trafalgar Square and built in 1824 by Smirke, now rebuilt as the Canada Building. It had been founded by the Duke of Wellington and Lord Castlereagh, and all its furniture, fittings and silver were of that fortunate date, also some of the servants liveries. The membership had, I gathered, become rather elderly and reduced in numbers by deaths, and it was suddenly realized that failing a quick transfusion of new young blood the club itself would die. This meant that instead of waiting on a candidate list perhaps for many years, as at most clubs worth joining, one might well get elected almost at once if acceptably proposed and seconded. This I contrived to do, and was well content until the First War came. It was well sited for state processions and I viewed that of King Edward's funeral, or George V's coronation (I forget which) in the utmost comfort. I had taken along with me a specification that I had to write, and that kept me happily busy throughout the day whilst we were all shut in until the show, of which I saw plenty, was safely over. But it was indeed a spectacle unlikely ever to be repeated.

When the 1914 War landed me in the Welsh Guards, joining the Guards Club—then at the entrance to Marlborough House (now replaced by the much better and vastly larger Midland Bank by Lutyens) was more or less automatic, and I continued to belong for some while after it had unwisely moved to larger premises in Brook Street and where, under the sanguine chairmanship of old General Sir John Ponsonby, I rather reluctantly served on the building committee that transformed the premises that had been impulsively bought into what the members were believed to want, but at crippling cost.

I had by this time been elected to the Athenaeum but after a while, feeling a bit too old for the Guards and really too young for the august Athenaeum, I compromised on the Travellers, where I had more friends than elsewhere. Elegant and excellent in every way, it was then certainly also a little dull, and such as sought my sponsorship for joining were, without exception, those of a hermit-like caste whose one aim was to withdraw and be let alone. I happened one day in the thirties to drop in to find the annual general meeting just beginning, with the chairman Lord Loch[1] about to address it, in effect thus:

> My lords and gentlemen, I am of course aware that one of the most cherished traditions of our club is that no member should ever accost another unless he happens to be a friend of his, apart from any fortuitous contact, within the Club. Nonetheless, I have to warn you that His Majesty's Government has asked me to extend our hospitality to certain distinguished official foreign guests for the occasion of the forthcoming Coronation. I suggest to you therefore that should any of you find yourselves sitting at table opposite any such, it would be courteous to pass the time of day with them. They will only be here for a very short time, and you will therefore be in no way committed. Thank you.

The 'No contact' rule really was observed most meticulously. For example Mr. Baldwin, the Prime Minister at the time,

[1] 2nd Baron Loch, d. 1942.

lunched at the Club almost every day at a table by himself with his nose in a 'Thriller', and though dozens of members besides myself must have at least met him outside the Club, I never, once, saw him greeted by or saw him speak to anyone. The taboo was so strong that when one day Lord Eustace Percy, who I knew well by sight (only) as being the then Minister for Education, sat down opposite to me at a table for two—we never exchanged a word throughout the meal though it was his own elder brother (Northumberland) who had actually proposed me for the Club. Phew!

Of course, all this kind of life depended on a, I suppose, unjustly exploited class of people: the servants. In the rather streamlined, self-service age in which we now live (I think I have only built one house since the war with a back staircase, once the requisite qualification of any 'authentic' mansion) it seems hard to believe that I do actually remember a grand old widow who lived alone in a fine great house, who entertained scarcely at all except for large pheasant shoots twice a year. In my mid-twenties, I attended one of these with an uncle of mine, who I think was her trustee. Anyway, I remember her complaining of her straitened circumstances. Having considered her sad plight, I well remember one of his suggestions for retrenchment:

'With so dependable a butler, is it really necessary to have *three* footmen?' Her perfectly serious response: 'Oh, I know it may *look* rather extravagant, but to be able to make up a four for whist in the pantry whenever they are all free does seem to make all the difference, and I do like to feel they are happy.' That, of course, was all before the First World War. During the Second, finding myself in another, far grander country house, Wentworth Woodhouse, (indeed about the most architecturally distinguished then still inhabited by its traditional family after I had converted Stowe into a public school) my hostess, Lady Fitzwilliam, said: 'I expect you would be interested by a bit of a look around, though with an infantry battalion and a headquarters staff sharing the house with us, I'm afraid I can't show you it all.' After some half-hour or so, while resting on a rather chilling marble seat somewhere amongst a lot of columns, I remarked that such a place must need quite a lot of servicing. 'Too true,' said my hostess, 'When we have it all to ourselves, we find we can't be really comfortable, with fewer than sixty-five indoors!' Still, if they were as kindly disposed towards their dependants as my poor widow, I daresay life below stairs was merry enough, if not adding significantly to the G.N.P. Those were certainly the days. Or were they?

To speak the truth, I am probably a little envious of some of today's freedoms, not imaginable in *my* day. Protocol was still terrific and strict chaperonage unrelaxed, and it was unthinkable that you should address any young lady unless you had been formally introduced by name by your hostess, her chaperone or a mutual friend. Though not a hunting man myself, with neither the time nor the money to indulge what had been my favourite boyhood sport, I was nonetheless somehow sucked into the Hunt Ball Circuit, and very jolly it was, my black dress coat not in the least abashed amongst all the hunting pink which, when also including the knee-breeches, silk stockings, buckled shoes and hunt emblems of the dressier clubs, seemed to waft one back to about Jane Austen's day, or beyond. The women's dresses, however fine they might be and their gala bast, were of the current fashion, whatever it might be and of no other period but their own, no doubt to be marvelled at and possibly admired again on T.V. screens by their great-great- grandchildren. One of the most prestigious of all these jolly occasions was nearing the uninhibited climax of its last proper dance before the terminal gallop, with Herr Stanislaw's band playing away as though inspired from on High, when, by some dire mischance, I found myself without a partner for this 'grande finale', my top favourite of all the current waltzes—'The Chocolate Soldier'. Alone against the end wall of the long ball-room I watched impatiently and beat time with my foot, morosely watching the rhythmic swirl of colour and exaltation sweep unfeelingly past. Then I suddenly realized I was *not* in fact alone but that a few yards away another wall-flower had materialized—a lovely girl whom I had often seen at other dances and much admired, but to whom I had never happened to be introduced—though I had learnt her name. Not in the least elevated by the evening's freely-flowing champagne (I am, as it happens, almost completely alcohol proof, which can sometimes be a drawback) I assumed that she would welcome a partner—any partner—as eagerly as I, and turned to her with 'A shame to miss this splendid last dance—what about it?' or something to that effect. Without even looking me reprovingly up and down, or speaking a word, she turned gracefully and walked away to remain a solitary spectator further along the same wall.

I would have cheerfully danced with a gorilla had one been available, and I guessed that she might be feeling the same, but nonetheless, propriety prevailed and there I stood, well and truly rebuffed. As a side-light on this already slightly eroded strictness of social intercourse, the sequel was significant. Not long after this strict lesson in correct deportment, I was invited to make one of a country-house party for another ball and whom should I find myself being formally presented to but my admired rejector of a few months earlier. She was all and more than I had guessed she might be, and now the ceremony of formal introduction having been duly performed, she was cordiality itself and we got along famously, though we neither of us referred to our embarrassing first encounter. I had reflected on the repressive strictures of the rules that had so tormentingly forbidden our enjoying each other's company sooner, but had come to realize that so very attractive a young girl might really need a bit of protection against 'unauthorized' attentions—for she would, quite apart from her own merits, have been quite a prize indeed for any unscrupulous adventurer, being as she was the eldest daughter and heiress apparent of a very senior and much respected earl of wide possessions. Long after this, I happened to find myself staying in the same country house as both her parents. They were themselves just as charming as I guessed they would be, but I was truly saddened to hear that their admirable daughter had died, I think as a Red Cross driver, in the First World War.

I recall one occasion at least when I was myself culpably careless of such conventions and reaped a just reward. Letters relevant to the affair ran thus:

(1)   *Him to Me:* (written from his Club)
      Sir—I am aware that last night you attended my wife's dance without being invited to do so, and I shall be glad of your explanation.

(2) *To which I replied:*
Sir—I must apologize for having unwittingly intruded where my presence was neither expected nor welcome, and then explain how it so unfortunately came about.

Some while ago I was kindly invited by Lady Blank to be a guest for a dinner party she was giving for your wife's ball, apparently at the suggestion of one of her other guests, as I did not really know her. However, I accepted and scribbled the fixture down in my pocket diary.

I was then informed that the dinner party had had to be cancelled, but not your wife's dance. I entirely accept that I received no invitation card to your wife's party—I wouldn't know, as I am afraid I am careless about such and have frequent purges, trusting to my diary to tell me where I am expected when. So please don't assume me to be an habitual gate-crasher, only an occasional muddle-head.

(3) *Him to Me:*
Dear Sir—Thank you for your letter, which certainly disposes of the matter in question satisfactorily. I only wish that I might have been better informed before I wrote to you as I did.

My general forgetfulness and mild disregard for social niceties came to be recognized and accepted as an unfortunate inborn trait and not a wilful flouting of convention. All the same, I would brace myself now and again, and go out of my way to proclaim my basic conformity to the current customs of the tribe, as when, at the end of one season, I hired a new-fangled and expensive taximeter cab, instead of a hansom (which would have taken too long) to run me hither and thither about London shedding the visiting cards that convention ordained it was proper to deposit at houses where one had been hospitably entertained in the recent past. Though I certainly shed a lot, I daresay a good many were at the wrong houses as my diary, like my memory, was never too reliable, but at the end of my expensive duty-drive I at least felt that for once I had done the correct thing—or tried to. There were, however, certain (or to me *un*certain) conventions about this strange card-bearing ceremonial that I never properly grasped or remembered. For instance, how many, under what circumstances and what exactly did the turning up of a corner signify, and when was *that* appropriate? I feel sure that I had been fully and kindly initiated into all such mysteries and niceties, but I could never remember, and I ought to have carried Lady Bell's entertaining little book, simply called *Etiquette* in my pocket, but I don't think it had yet been published.

I first met Lady Bell staying in the country with Mrs. Humphrey Ward for a large weekend party, and somehow discovering that she was an old friend of the Stracheys, I did all I could to entertain her and ingratiate myself in the hope that she might act as a bridge to give me readier access to Amabel (Strachey) whom I had just begun to court. Lady Bell herself was a most splendid and cultivated old lady, who gave frequent literary-political parties at her London house in Sloane Street, and indeed ran a regular 'salon' of which her entertaining little etiquette book, though thoroughly informative and indeed authoritative, was by no means typical, but a light-hearted squib to help such as myself and save us from making unnecessary mistakes, and to inform us of the accepted conventions of current society, however foolish they might seem. She warmed my heart by praising Amabel in general and her intelligence in particular, and did act her allotted part as a bridge with her accustomed tact and expertise. She was generally so encouraging that I went for a long tramp the following day, Sunday, with her son-in-law Sir Charles Trevelyan. I talked to him mostly about marriage, sought his advice on all manner of more or less relevant subjects, and was no doubt intolerably boring, as those in my then condition are apt to be. However, in all the circumstances that I loaded him with, and those that he anyhow knew, his advice was an unequivocal: 'Go right ahead and win her if you can,' and so it was, and so I did.   And now it suddenly strikes me that without the hospitality of the formidable yet most kindly Mrs. Humphrey Ward—a sort of literary Queen Victoria at that time—I might never have braced myself to propose to Amabel, in which sad case I feel pretty sure that I should have found myself this evening still a bachelor, if alive at all, and writing, if at all, far less cheerfully.

II

Around the Mediterranean

One spring in the early 1960s, we chartered an elegant English yacht the *Oronsay* at Monaco—a 30-ton schooner—and set sail in moonlight with a light breeze to make a night passage to Corsica. There we arrived off the exquisite little port of Calvi in a rosy dawn—the aromatic scent of the island having long preceded our sighting of it. With us as our guests were Lionel and Christian Brett[1] and Elizabeth Beazley[2]—all of us acting as crew under our most expert and amiable skipper, a somewhat Conrad-like character as ready to discuss the writings of Marcel Proust as great-circle navigation. Though fire had recently devastated some of the forests, we found the island, its villages and flowers entrancing and, of course, all chose the old houses that we would certainly try to buy and one day return to.

Eastwards on to Elba, partly propelled thereto by A. P. Herbert's book on Napoleon's exile, which happened to be in the ship's bookshelf. Therein he maintained that had he not been

---

[1] Viscount and Viscountess Esher, he an architect, she a painter.
[2] Now Mrs. Walters, architect and author.

so shabbily treated by the victorious alliance, the Emperor would have been perfectly content to remain in his idyllic little kingdom and carry on with the enlightened programmes for improvements and reforms of all sorts that he had so imaginatively launched. It is certainly a thought, but I wonder. Assuredly, *I* should have been supremely happy there, or I think I should, but then the Emperor and I have nothing whatever in common save this one urge towards town and country planning.

After a somewhat rough day's sailing, we decided to seek a quiet night's rest in the snug little harbour of a small island called (I think) Caprira. As we warped in to the quay, we were shouted at by a surprisingly unwelcoming official who (as none of us knew enough Italian) we entirely failed to understand. However, through shouts and gestures it eventually emerged that he wanted the captain (only) to come ashore with the ship's papers and all passports. After a long wait our skipper returned with the unexpected news that we must none of us on any account land, because, so it transpired, the island was a most strictly guarded penal colony, where we had no right to put in anyway.

He had, however, gained a concession (I think by somehow inducing the harbour master to telephone the governor). We would be graciously permitted to stay tied up where we were until the morning. Even this minimal privilege had had apparently to be fought for inch by inch, and only won when our undefeatable envoy had represented us as being personages of the utmost distinction, Lionel as an English noble of the highest rank (though he had yet to succeed to his father's peerage) and myself as a 'Commendatore' (which seemed to have some Italian significance) on the mere strength of my C.B.E.

We half expected a visit aboard from the suspicious harbour master when the champagne bottle we opened at dinner to celebrate Amabel's birthday (that gives me the date, the tenth of May, but not the year) produced the loudest gunlike bang I have ever heard—from a cork—perhaps due to the excessive resonance of our panelled saloon—or maybe the wine itself (secretly purchased on Corsica by our guests) was unuaully explosive.

We had a spanking sail on to Elba and around the great cliff that hides and protects its secret and most beautiful harbour from the open sea. We stayed there as long as we could, exploring the lovely island and examining the Napoleonic buildings and relics. We were sorry to leave but our yacht's charter was only for a fortnight. On up the coast of Italy, when a sudden and quite severe gale (a kind known locally as the 'Libeccio') forced us to heave-to and then run back almost under bare poles as far as we had sailed that day, thankful to make the shelter of Savona, a most interesting old town with arcaded streets that no-one seems to visit or even know of, simply because it is a commercial port without a *plage* or other popular tourist attractions. We were gratified to find our brief ordeal reported on the radio and, with much embellishment, in the local press. I was later somewhat teased by my shipmates when, on our skipper's orders to fasten our life-lines, I had abstractedly clipped mine to the handle to a great iron butane gas cylinder on the deck, with which, had the worst happened, as it seemed it might, I would have inevitably plummeted straight to the bottom. But it didn't, so I didn't.

On up the coast to Carrara with its famous marble quarries which, alas, we just had not time enough to visit, and then on again to Portofino whose intimate little toy harbour Lionel was all against our entering as he said I should be disillusioned after forty years—the most notable church had been destroyed by bombing though rebuilt, and the whole place now seethed with tourists and their coaches, the shops displaying nothing but picture-postcards and loathsome souvenirs. It certainly sounded dismal enough, but I could not find myself so near my once-beloved without a passing salutation. And in truth it was essentially still my Portofino, on which legend will insist (and falsely) that I modelled Portmeirion. Fortunately Mussolini had had it declared a National Monument so that architecturally at least its integrity is (I hope) assured.

So happy had we been with the *Oronsay* and her skipper and our Mediterranean cruise generally, that we decided to repeat it the following May, this time joining the yacht at Messina with the aim of circumnavigating Sicily east about. We took with us the Philip Hugh-Joneses and completed our circuit of the island in precisely the fourteen days of our charter, to the very hour, though not without incidents. It was a most agreeable way of sightseeing—fanning out inland from successive ports of call to see the many 'musts' in the way of classical remains—theatres, temples and museums—and musts they certainly were.

We took due note of Garibaldi's doings; drank admirable Marsala *in* Marsala, and made a dash for the town of Noto from a port in which we were sheltering from so violent a gale that we only dared to leave the yacht unattended after we had run out no less than ten warps to make sure of holding her. I had been especially looking forward to seeing Noto, as a completely Baroque town raised in the late-eighteenth century on the site of its mediaeval predecessor that had been entirely destroyed by an earthquake. But the small snapshots that I had happened across had misled me and raised expectations that the reality failed to fulfil. The detail was repetitive and coarse, the stone-work a uniform and unpleasing ginger-brown, the iron-work feeble, and the whole layout perfunctory. Altogether a sad let-down when I had been boosting it as *the* plum of our whole cruise. I rather meanly wrote a denigrating piece about it in *Country Life* where another contributor had just been lauding its distinction.

But we were generously compensated by a quite unforeseen treat in the shape of the minute little hill-top town of Erice, normally reached by a cable-way which, however, was out of action because of the high wind—so up the looping zig-zag road we climbed by taxi, to eat a memorable lunch in its miniature piazza with what one might call 'about an hour's worth' of architecture and town-planning close around us, the diameter of the whole place from edge to edge being no more than a few hundred yards.

Ever since I first read Norman Douglas's *South Wind* I had dreamed of one day visiting Capri and savouring the reality of the island about which he had woven his magical story. Quite early the novelist Brett-Young had invited me to stay with them there, but I couldn't get away then, and later when I might have done so, all the knowledgeable said that now it was far too late, the island had been ruined by mass popularity and that I should be lucky not to be trampled to death. Not so James (now Jan) Morris,[1] who had lately been there in connection with his great *Pax Britannica* trilogy, who advised that for *me* at any rate, it was still most abundantly worth while and that out of full season the place was still peaceful, still charming.

Arriving there in early May 1967, we found him entirely right. Everything had just opened, but hardly any visitors had yet arrived and we wandered about the enticing and scrupulously clean little town and its adjoining coast and countryside almost as though they had been specially reserved for our own unaccompanied and leisurely perambulation. Indeed I found it a sort of Portmeirion writ large, but with perpetual high water lapping its rock-bound tideless shores. We had introductions to various hospitable residents but there were other places I wanted to see, especially the spectacular coastline towards Amalfi and beyond, which was a day-long trip by steamer and bus, and scenically most rewarding. At one point along the Corniche road there is a lay-by and a lift descending to sea-level where a blue grotto can be explored by boat. That of Capri (which we had all to ourselves with a friendly old boatman who had rowed us right round the island) had sufficiently whetted my appetite for such phenomena, so down I went.

I walked into the dark mouth of the cave from the rock platform and almost instantly found myself gasping under water, having stepped off the rock edge straight into the sea. With myself, my clothes, wallet and watch all dripping cold sea water, on my way to a luncheon party at Amalfi, I was a little stern with the grotto's guardians for providing no rail or white line or light or warning of any sort, when even the clear-sighted such as myself become instantly and utterly blind in the almost complete darkness of the cave after the dazzling sunshine without. I plugged my venerable age, my recent coronary, and that it was extremely lucky for them that they were not landed with a corpse which might well have proved embarrassing to explain away. They seemed to agree that my complaints were just and that precautions should certainly be taken. I wonder if they have been.

We were a party of only three or four in charge of a charming

[1] Travel writer, author of *Venice*, and *Oxford*.

and intelligent girl courier who acted as interpreter—only giving
us information when asked for it, and that with clarity and
humour. She took entire charge of me after my ducking, being
greatly and unnecessarily concerned about 'delayed shock'—
organized the drying of my clothes in a little nearby café where
I could collect them on the way back from Amalfi, and meanwhile borrowed odds and ends for me that would at least serve
the cause of decency, most memorably a pair of check chef's
trousers, immensely roomy but far too short, that I hoped the
head waiter of the hotel where we were due to lunch would
accept as merely eccentric and not insulting. He apparently did.

Naples was unavoidable as a base, not only for Capri and the
other attractive islands that we briefly visited, but also for the
great Palace of Caserta that I had always wanted to visit ever
since I had passed low over it on some long-ago flight and recognized its layout from remembered plans and photographs. But it is
far too large in scale and a little too late in date to be really
pleasing. Indeed, transcending the human scale so arrogantly, it
was all rather intimidating as was perhaps its relatively   in-
significant royal builder's intention. Even its vast park and
insistently formal gardens are beyond the compass of most
present day legs, and you need a cab to see them without undue
fatigue. Still quantitatively at least, it does deserve its celebrity
as one of the world's wonders, like it or not. Naples, on the
contrary, now creeping untidily out towards Caserta as well as
along its once famous bay in both directions, we found utterly
repellent. True, it can offer certain isolated buildings and institutions of interest—its marine laboratory for instance, but as a
great city it seemed to us completely unfit for human habitation
with a traffic problem that looked insoluble—and probably is.
The trouble is that towns do not commit actual suicide by self-
strangulation and start afresh; they tend to struggle wretchedly
on, half paralysed. For Naples, Vesuvius may now hold the only
solution, as it did for Pompeii.

A fairly recent trip abroad has been a return visit to Corsica
where I had a professional appointment to keep, and at the
moment of writing I am grumpily inclined to hope it may be our
last, as we were caught on the island by the French General

Strike which vastly multiplied and magnified all the delays, waitings and arrangement-making incidental to most travel, to which I am anyhow almost morbidly allergic. For sheer drama, I doubt whether the serrated and contorted pinnacles of the Corsican highlands can be beaten for form or colour anywhere, and the roads that contrive to thread their wriggling way between them, along precipices, across gorges, through chestnut groves and mighty pine forests, are miracles of vertiginous engineering. The intrepid Amabel wanted to hire a drive-yourself car for our explorations, but on such roads you either keep your eyes steadily ahead and away from the surrounding landscape or you perish down a precipice. The hazard is, of course, increased by one's instinctive 'wrong side' driving, and the confident brink-manship of the impetuous native drivers.

For so comparatively short and simple an expedition, this Corsican trip was really wonderfully bedevilled by mischances. Arrived at the Kensington air terminal in good time for our early morning flight direct to Ajaccio, for which we had prudently booked long ahead, we were blandly informed that it had been cancelled, and that there were no others that would get us to Corsica that day via anywheresoever. The best offer was a flight in a few hours' time to Paris where, next morning, we could catch that day's plane for the island. We thought that we rather disliked Paris, but it was a warm and radiant May day with the chestnuts just out and after booking in at a snug little hotel a hundred yards from Les Invalides Terminal, we set out to 'do' the architectural heart of Paris thoroughly, and so perhaps to revise our rather jaundiced views, which indeed we did. First, an open-deck launch trip along the Seine and around the Isle de France and back, which I had somehow never done before, then in the brilliant late afternoon light, a leisurely perambulation round the Rue de Rivoli and Place Vendome, which was by then almost empty of all traffic and even of pedestrians, so that one could wander around at will admiring the chaste detailing of now cleansed stonework that was a revelation. Then, as the sun was setting behind the Arc de Triomphe, a shaft of golden light beating down the splendid vista of the Tuilleries Gardens to illumine the Louvre buildings as dramatically as though skilfully floodlit. Driving back after dinner, we called in on our old friend Madame Benda[1] who brought us up to date on the Sorbonne students' demonstration which had lately begun. We were of course aware of it, but had seen nothing and never guessed what it would lead to, the French General Strike, that was to shatter our programme.

Having finished our planned Corsican reconnaissance (that included certain coastal preservation ploys) we said good-bye to our excellent Ajaccio 'Hotel des Etrangers' and drove off to the airport, only to be confronted by the notice 'All Flights Cancelled'. We had followed the course of events in France on television, which however had been vaguely reassuring so that this was a facer, as I had fixtures to keep at home. We had however spotted a fine looking steamer *Le Napoleon* in Ajaccio harbour on our way to the airport, which our taximan (who had driven us about the island) told us would be sailing for Marseilles that evening. So back to Ajaccio full speed to secure berths—the last-available—and of course only in an extravagant *cabin de luxe*. However, anything to reach the mainland we thought, as a first homeward step but, being Sunday, just everything in Marseilles was shut and there was nothing for it but to eat and sleep and sight-see until (we hoped) Monday morning would open up *some* office that could tell us something. Meantime, we thoroughly explored the old harbour, drove out to quiz Le Corbusier's so famous 'Unité d'Habitation' which I found slightly easier to take than I had expected, despite its coarse texture and depressing colour. We thereafter ascended to the dreadful dominating Cathedral of Notre Dame, which made me almost thankful for Corbusier. But it gives one a wide birds-eye view over the whole sprawling city that, since the Germans demolished the intricate and notoriously picturesque waterside warrens that I remembered and that proved so useful to the slippery Resistance, has little now beyond its two fine harbours either to interest or impress one.

Monday morning's enquiry at the tourist bureau brought no cheer at all—no planes, no trains, no ships, no buses. Nothing for it but an appeal to our British Consul who was instantly alert and helpful. 'Look, if you could get round here with your luggage

[1] Widow of J. Benda, author of *le trahison des clevcs*.

Plate 5a   The *Oronsay* (foreground) moored in the harbour at Portofino

Plate 5b   Port Grimaud

G. Livingstone Evans, 15 *Church Street, Blaenau Ffestiniog*

Plate 6a   Rhiwlas, near Bala, a new manor house in the local vernacular

G. Livingstone Evans, 15 *Church Street, Blaenau Ffestiniog*

Plate 6b   The Cliff House, the latest addition at Portmeirion

within twenty minutes, I will try and get you on to a private strike-breaking bus that I have managed to get hold of to run other stranded English across France and into Switzerland—can you make it?' Somehow, by a wild scramble, we did, only to find that the driver of the promised bus had funked the black-leg job and not shown up. However, after a long wait another excellent bus did appear and off we set, but with small hope now of catching the Geneva-to-London night flight on which our Consul had booked us places. Our travelling companions were mostly a charming party of bird-watchers who had been innocently isolated with their flamingoes in the Carmargue, blithely unaware of any snags obstructing their return. As they seemed to be largely university dons and school teachers and elderly ladies—none of them well off—I think our Consul must have given or lent them the money for the unforeseen expenses of the bus ride and emergency flight home which were quite substantial—as we found. In writing him an ordinary cheque for our air fare and paying him in francs for the bus ride, I asked 'What if we couldn't have paid?' 'Well,' he said, 'we would have got you home all the same—cheaper far, you know, than keeping you here.' Comforting.

We were scarcely clear of the wide flung sprawl of Marseilles itself before we were into the disorderly ribbon-built chaos of somewhere else and indeed it was pleasanter *not* to look out of the windows until we reached the foothills of the Haute Savoie where narrow defiles with their precipitous cliffs and forests defied impertinent interference. Yet, wherever opportunity offered, the infection seemed to recur even over the Swiss border where I had hoped for some relief from disfigurement. Of personal relief we had none, save at one brief halt in our eight-hour ride where we queued up at a wayside bar to snatch buttered rolls.

At the frontier we had a long hold-up as our party by now somehow included a young Yugoslav couple, whose papers were deemed not to be in order, which meant our hanging impatiently about whilst the irregularity was referred to higher authority. On our eventually reaching Geneva airport, our intended plane, no doubt tired of waiting for more than the forty minutes grace it had promised us, had taken off. However, the (again admirable)

G

Consular official who had been alerted to meet us said there was a later flight, but two seats short for our whole party. Having adequate funds in hand ourselves, we volunteered to be left behind, and put up at a surprisingly tatty and un-Swiss-like hotel adjoining the air terminal until the next morning's flight ended our small adventures. Our heterogeneous party thus fortuitously flung together to face an unforeseen emergency irresistibly suggested the opening of some corny old novel where our gay young Yugoslavs would certainly have been sinister, the grumbling and boringly talkative American woman who knew no-one and was shunned by all would be the obvious destined murderee, whilst the handsome young man who acted as general shepherd to the whole party by tacit consent would inevitably have been cast as hero.

On a recent trip to Tunisia, we were much impressed by its government's determination to prevent the disastrous squandering of its attractive coastline as has been so thoughtlessly allowed on too much of the Mediterranean seaboard—most notoriously in France and Spain, with Greece (it is to be feared) only too anxious recklessly to cash in on tourism in the same short-sighted way. Greece, of course, after its internal political distractions is now no doubt poorer than ever and that much more eager for foreign currency from tourist development, at no matter what ultimate cost to the country's scenic integrity— every innocent little Greek island and bay seeming now to be offering itself for prostitution.

Not so Tunisia, where Hammamet is typical of much intelligent, far-sighted and quite new coastal development—a great sickle of a sandy bay guarded by an ancient little Arab walled town and castle on a rocky headland at one extremity. Back behind the sand-dunes and their own fine trees and gardens are strung some half-dozen long, low, luxurious modern hotels, architecturally acceptable in themselves as exemplary in their courteous self-effacement, whereby the splendid bay itself is left still virgin and scarcely aware of the developed hinterland. At one end of this so discreetly marshalled line of hotels stands a little white domed and vaulted palace with colonnaded marble swimming pool and loggias in the midst of a great garden that it shares with an impressive new open-air theatre which Elizabeth Taylor had recently graced, that had every kind of up-to-date equipment. We had heard of this delectable establishment—a government 'Cultural Centre'—from Teddy Wolfe[1] who had spent a fortnight painting there, and through the Cultural Attache at the Tunisian Embassy in London, and ours in Tunis, we contrived to be lodged there for a few blissful days. We had the whole place entirely to ourselves except for its attentive staff and a fleeting young American 'Peace Corps' architect measuring up for proposed extensions—his rucksack stuffed full with the works of Lewis Mumford, which was entirely as it should be.

[1] Edward Wolfe, R.A.

12

The Miracle of Port Grimaud

It is possible, and indeed I think probable, that the founding within the last decade, and now near completion of the little town of Port Grimaud on the French Mediterranean sea-board may prove to be the most hopeful and significant architectural and planning achievement of our time. It is at the head of the gulf of St. Tropez, occupying a featureless sandy salt marsh, where a few sheep and long-obsolete evaporating pans for salt gave the desolate area its only visible value.

It was this virgin gap in the almost continuous mis-exploitation of the whole Cote d'Azur that François Spoerry had known as a bird-watching and sketching boy and where, as a young architect, he returned to take a leading part in the local Resistance when the Germans took over during the last war. With his satchel full of archaeological books and plans and sketches of ancient ruins and birds, he was for quite a while accepted as no more than an eccentric and quite harmless youth, ready enough to talk, but only about his own special subjects. His joining up with a group of genuine archaeologists camping in the remote and splendid ruins of the Chartreuse Notre Dame De La Verne to make an official record, gave young Francois plausible extra cover for his clandestine Resistance activities.

In the end, however, some leak or other somewhere gave him away, and he was well and truly 'processed' by the Gestapo. Fortunately for him, Spoerry was a fluent talker and story-teller with a remarkable memory so that he was able to escape actual torture by volunteering all sorts of plausible false information—stuff that *he* knew *they* knew already—an apparently intelligent if uncautious young man who might yet let out something of some use to his captors. So he was kept (more or less) alive in a succession of concentration camps until he found himself at last in the notorious death camp of Dachau. There, however, he was detailed for work in the kitchens where a strict starvation diet could not be easily enforced. Whence, by this happy chance, he was able to repair his skeletal body and emerge in tolerable condition when the camp was captured by the advancing Americans.

A free man at last, and with his 'Beaux Arts' architectural degree behind him—he was soon back in his own world again of architecture and design generally, and with special reference to his own native Provence. Naturally, his thoughts turned to the still virgin Grimaud marshlands that he had known so well and that no-one else seemed to have thought about, whilst the rest of the poor old Cote d'Azur was being packed ever tighter with building developments large and small, wastefully jostling one another, to no coherent plan, for a glimpse of the fabled Mediterranean. Spoerry saw the wasteful and disfiguring folly of all this 'beggar my neighbour' mis-development, and resolved to show the way to something better that would not only enhance the natural amenities of its setting but also prove profitable. Having thoroughly prospected the whole available area, probed the subsoil, checked the river's flow and the tidal range, the impact of the Mistral winds from the adjoining mountains, he bought the land at its low agricultural value and proceeded to draft successive ingenious plans for its development.

Very odd-looking indeed were his successive lay-out schemes—

more like the outline of some mis-shapen octopus than the plan
for a seriously intended town. But when you realized that the
head of the creature represented the sheltered harbour and the
river's mouth, and that the tentacles, twisting this way and that,
were the sea-water thoroughfares, you began to see daylight and
to appreciate the extreme ingenuity of the whole concept—a
town where all the main thoroughfares are canals and its squares
and *grandes places* lagoons; all the traffic by boat, launch or yacht
if not on foot, with cars parked unobtrusively without the main
entrance gateway.

Of course, the unique peace and beauty of the whole place,
which one now relishes so keenly, had to be preceded by several
years of intense and noisy engineering activity, whilst great
machines excavated the underlying sand with drag lines to create
the water-ways, and piled it up behind sheet-piling to form the
promontories, islands and isthmuses that carry the buildings and
their land approaches. Then M. Spoerry the civil engineer,
handed over to M. Spoerry the architect, landscape designer and
artist, who proceeded to clothe his skeletal framework with
an altogether captivating dress of endlessly variegated houses,
terraces, shops, hotels, restaurants, offices and the rest, that,
of all sorts and sizes and colours, nonetheless blend into a total
picture that is entirely satisfying and pleasurable, both in mass
and in detail.

Nearly every house has its own little patio garden and its
landing stage, where its own boat or small yacht can be moored
and public transport is supplied by elegant canopied motor barges
that ply from quay to quay throughout the day. All the public
services are laid on—including T.V. and radio from some distant
receiver—sewage is pumped to a treatment works far away and
all the town's waterways are as limpidly clear as the open sea,
whose twelve inch tide keeps them as inviting for swimmers as
for fish. Each of the hundreds of houses differ subtly from each
other, though they are all roofed with the same robust, reddish
pantiles traditional to the district, laid over waterproofed concrete, proof even against a cloudburst driven almost horizontally
by the gales that can sometimes lash down from the mountains
at over a hundred miles an hour. Though here and there there

are occasional prim little terraces of matching houses, individuality is the keynote of all other building, great or small, high or low, mostly stuccoed over brickwork and colour-washed from a wide palette that ranges through the whole spectrum from white to ox-blood red, giving the effect of a most subtly colour-conscious citizenry, whereas every single house has its colour chosen for it by M. Spoerry himself, and must stay so for ever, though the owner is free to modify and decorate the interior of his house to suit himself. His gardening too is his own affair, and the way in which he has embellished his little plots with flowers, creepers, vine trellis, shrubs and even trees, shows his proper pride not only for his individual dwelling but for the total impact of his unique town.

All the houses are sold freehold, and I have never seen one empty or to let, though doubtless some are, when the owners are elsewhere, whether cruising in their yachts or earning their livings. For Port Grimaud has, and deservedly, apparently now become one of the most sought-after yacht harbours of the whole Mediterranean, and at the season's end both the official Marina and most of the various quays are close-packed with elegant vessels, large and small, from single-handed little sloops and cutters to great ocean-going square-sail schooners. With all but these last mostly built of white fibreglass, decks, cabin tops and all, and now invariably with tall, slender, shining tubular aluminium masts, the 'laying up' winter season has its own special interest, as one can spend days just quizzing craft of every sort, from all over the world, assessing sea-keeping qualities and the personalities of their owners.

M. Spoerry has built his own most ingeniously elegant house at the very end of a spit of land that commands the entrance to his town from the harbour at the river's mouth—so that every vessel arriving or departing, manoeuvres, well or ill, under his critical eye, for he is an experienced and dedicated sailor himself, when not absorbed in architecture and the planning of further new towns, which is all more than enough for an ordinary man. Indeed, with all his multifarious interests, skills and responsibilities, one has to face the fact that he is *not* an ordinary man. Whether as civil engineer, architect, town-planner, land-developer, financier, gadgeteer, administrator or artist, he is also and above all, literally a man of *vision*.

Often beginning with doodle free-hand sketches, a layout pattern will emerge which will be gradually elaborated into a definite project, to be further altered and refined until he is reasonably satisfied that he has 'got it'. Then he will have an accurate small-scale wooden model made and photographed in different lights from all directions, and if he is not completely satisfied that he has done the best he can, he makes the alterations that he judges will give him the effect he is aiming at. I don't know, but I suspect that at some stage he tries different colours on his models and then has them re-photographed standing on a mirror, as entrancing reflections are a very important part of the whole place's enchantment. He is a great one for arched gateways and elegant humped-back bridges, both fully justified by practical considerations, and for occasional towers or bastions in splendid solid masonry as (visibly) necessary foils to less substantial structures. How much the creator of this place saw of all this enchanting detail in his mind's eye when he set about his excavations, I don't know, but I guess a good deal of it—for the unexpected and always rewarding glimpses, framed between A and B of distant C are just the sort of views one would have invented for oneself if they had not been ready made for one. If there is anything wrong in building pictures instead of painting them, why then M. Spoerry is a sinner indeed, and if condemned by the architectural establishment to be hanged, I should be proud to hang beside him.

There is always something new and admirable to rejoice over. Since my last visit a year or two ago, beside his own presiding residence, the place's 'Doge's Palace' as it were, a really noble multi-denominational church has shot up on the little island reached by a monumental bridge from the end of the market place, to accompany the Town Hall already established there. It is the only modern church I have found myself really able to admire—original, elegant, yet impressively substantial, with great battered buttresses, a heavy pan-tiled, low-pitched roof behind its parapets, and a flat topped high tower with a single big bell within an iron-work cage on top. The tower's flat top is accessible as a public viewing platform through an outside turn-stile. Certainly it serves that secondary purpose well, but though the outlook is certainly wide and impressive, I still find it inadequate, and the one addition to the town's generous amenities that I have been badgering Spoerry to provide, is a still higher tower at some suitable central spot, topped with a camera obscura which would give the viewer a bird's eye picture of the whole immensely intricate complex. If even little Portmeirion can provide such an instructive and entertaining amenity, Port Grimaud deserves one a hundred times over.

M. Spoerry is a loyal Provencal and feels that any sort of tall slim tower would look too like an Italian Campanile and be alien to the whole spirit of the place. Maybe he is right, he generally is, but all the same, when he next comes to Port-meirion, his own creation's elder (but still baby) brother, I shall rub his nose in my own little tower, contrived from the peri-scope of a salvaged enemy submarine of the First World War. Apart from that, I can think of nothing that could add more to the allure of Port Grimaud. Refined gold needs no gilding, and François Spoerry's lily no painting beyond his own. If it be grumpily objected that Port Grimaud, like Portmeirion, is of no significance, as being 'merely' places for pleasurable relaxation—the same would go for Bath and for Brighton, where a scrupulous care for their lay-out, architecture and amenities has given them a survival value that go-as-you-please developments are unlikely to enjoy.

Blackpools may be inevitable and doubtless have their own special attractions for their vast and faithful clienteles, and it will probably always be a minority who have dreams of Xanadus and seek some contemporary reminder, however, faint, of that fabled pleasaunce. That the Port Grimaud triumph is no flash-in-the-pan architectural bonanza but a perfectly logical and viable town-planning exemplar for the almost tideless Mediterranean would seem proved by the fact that with government backing, its creator was commissioned to plan a whole multi-purpose coastal city of some 30,000 inhabitants near Toulon, opposite the delectable St. Hier group of little islands. Apart from the com-mercial and yacht harbour, an airport and rail terminal near the industrial area are provided for; all governmental, municipal and administrative buildings being clustered on their own spacious island and the whole city plan with its winding waterways, its connecting bridges and open spaces (its lagoon) being reminiscent of its smaller prototype.

The site for this ambitious large-scale experiment is singularly like that of the original triumph, deserted salt marsh and all, but with the advantage of a sheltering belt of flourishing Mediterranean pines just back from its sandy shore. Having studied the most ingenious draft plans for this splendid architectural adventure with rising enthusiasm, I dearly hoped that I might live long enough to see at least part of its actual realisation. But first the French General Strike and then the assorted political and financial crises have supervened to damp down government enterprise of this sort, and unless it recovers its nerve sooner than looks likely at the moment, I doubt whether, at ninety-four, I can hang on long enough even to applaud the preliminary excavations. But whether soon or late, I shall leave it all my humble blessing.

13

Portmeirion Grows Up

Insofar as I may hereafter be remembered at all, I expect it would be rather as the founder and creator of Portmeirion than for any other reason—if only because it has been evolving for so long— half a century—and because it is so much more *me* than anything else I have built elsewhere. I have always been more interested in the *grouping* of buildings than in the individual structures however prestigious, and a perfect site for a demonstration of my theories and fancies on a lovely peninsula almost on my doorstep proved irresistible. Though it has all been the utmost fun, and not merely for myself but also, as it has proved, for numberless others, I did have several perfectly serious purposes in doing what I did.

I wanted to show that one could develop even a very beautiful site without defiling it and indeed, given sufficient sympathy and skill, one might even enhance what nature had provided as your background. *Second*, I was saddened at finding so many people missing the intense interest and enjoyment to be gained from an appreciation of architecture, landscape, design, the use of colour and perspectives, and indeed of the environmental arts generally—often, I found, because they were shy of technicalities—so I sought to provide an easy, gay, sort of 'light opera' approach to these seeming mysteries, that would not frighten them off but entice them into interest, criticism and finally enjoyment. Finally, having seen so many potentially hopeful projects fail to fulfil their promoter's hopes and promises through architectural and planning ineptitude—I hoped to suggest that architectural good manners *can* mean good business.

As for most other enterprises almost everywhere, the Second World War proved the great divide, with re-thinking and often re-direction essential for survival. This was manifestly true of Portmeirion which had previously relied on the relatively restricted patronage of the well-to-do intelligentsia, a large proportion of whom were annual 'regulars'. Their reduced effective incomes and the inevitably increased cost of catering for them naturally meant the shrinking of the hotel's hitherto ample bookings. So, in 1953, when building could again take place, the fundamental question was: Could Portmeirion survive at all, or if it could, could it do so with sufficient vitality to pay for its own growth, as it had in the pre-war period?

The conclusion arrived at was that if our former patronage could no longer fully support the place, there would have to be an infusion of newcomers who could; provisions would have to be made for a new, wider and different public. This justified, and indeed demanded, increased accommodation, meaning the very welcome enlargement of the village along the lines originally envisaged, and a general improvement and extension of all essential services. Repairs, replacements, of carpets, furniture and fittings, and maintenance generally had of necessity been minimal throughout the War and its immediate aftermath, and the list of urgently needed works was formidable indeed, and all at enormously risen costs. Probably it was just as well that I had no idea at the time just how much relatively unproductive, from an architectural point of view, and certainly unshowy, expenditure would have to be undertaken: kitchens, drains, electricity supplies, all had to be renewed or replaced and twenty or thirty private bathrooms added.

This sort of change had always been foreseen as a not unlikely possibility, and there were numerous alternative draft plans for further buildings from which to pick those that would best provide the extra accommodation called for, whilst at the same time filling in the originally imagined total picture. It was not at all a matter of matching up with the earlier structures but rather of providing piquant contrasts whereby both old and new would gain in interest. Thus, where I judged that I had perhaps a trifle overplayed the picturesque, I would pop in a bland facade of serene classical formality: for example, the village aspect of the Bridge House as seen beyond the shamelessly picturesque front of the black weather-boarded Pilot House. In the same manner the Palladian Gloriette vivaciously contradicts the more sober, old, converted stable block across the way.

Many, but not all, of the earlier cottages originally built chiefly to provide extra accommodation for the hotel guests have now been modified and thoroughly re-equipped to provide elegant and convenient self-service units for which the demand seems to be ever increasing. Several units closest to the hotel are still retained for its direct letting and have their own devotees who book their accustomed quarters there year after year. Some cottages that were previously available for letting have now been withdrawn and pretty thoroughly modernised and re-serviced to provide really attractive quarters for an increased number of now more and more sophisticated resident staff, providing the village with a properly indigenous population.

Day visitors have come to play an increasingly important part in the development of Portmeirion, for while adequate provision had to be made for their amusement and enjoyment, the privacy and quiet of the 'resident' had also to be remembered. Thus, outlying parts of the village and the area around the hotel, have been closed off for 'hotel residents only' while in the centre of the village which is open to all, there is a natural and desirable hum of business and acitivity giving colour and atmosphere to the scene. The needs of day visitor and resident alike can be met in the various shops where goods are specially chosen to be of a high standard of craftsmanship, and more pressing requirements in the self-service cafeteria or bars. There is much to look at and explore, in the Gwyllt and the Peninsula gardens as well as in the village itself, enough to keep most interested and curious people happy for their whole day out. A new and greatly increased car park has had to be added but it is as pleasantly tree-screened as the old one that it supplements, although it has necessitated new and much improved traffic arrangements whereby cars and pedestrians are separated to the greater comfort and safety of both.

It would be generally conceded that places can be as widely different in their characters as are people. What is particularly gratifying about the still-evolving Portmeirion is the way in which it has gradually become, as I had hoped, a now widely recognised and welcoming centre for social occasions of every sort, from gala balls and local celebrations to the conferences of learned, cultural and professional societies, many of whose members become 'regulars'. It is no doubt the re-erected seventeenth-century Hercules Hall, part of the so-called Town Hall Complex, which is the chief magnet attracting such gatherings, as well as exhibitions and specialized fairs. Sometimes the whole place is wide open for charity fetes or organized festivals for children, or, for their elders, music and fireworks after nightfall. The Portmeirion Carnival has now become a much enjoyed annual event, with its own 'Queen' and attendant celebrations. Much of this I had dreamt, but never seriously expected to see in my own lifetime, as even my own invented name 'Portmeirion' had not appeared on any map until printed large and clear on one prepared by the Germans for our invasion and sent me from the battlefront. That our mere existence should be acknowledged at that early stage was encouraging, if only by a sworn enemy.

Now that the whole complex, though still miniature, seems to have been pushed and pulled into really viable shape through more than half a century of trial and error, it does seem to have settled down now into what should remain its future and permanent state, though with the almost endless opportunities offered by the Gwyllt and the woodlands and exotic jungles of the peninsula, it could well go on growing for generations. Watchful maintenance is of course assumed as well as discretion in the acceptance of even the most tempting offers of more architectural

monuments and fragments. Two most prestigious of these latter
have been donated this very year, from Westminster Abbey and
St. Paul's, the former already most aptly making its contribution
to the scene, whilst a worthy site already awaits the latter.

No buildings, as yet, have been imported from abroad, but
outlandish foreigners unexpectedly turning up at Portmeirion,
speaking no tongue known to someone of the pretty language-
conscious staff, are by no means unknown—but the most exotic
and lovely visitor we ever had was speechless and unable to
explain her arrival, having died almost on our threshold. She
was *Thunnus Albacarus*, otherwise a most lovely yellow-finned
tropical Tuna Fish, clad in a shimmering sheath of silvery scales,
some six feet long, weighing four hundred pounds, and left
stranded on a sand bank by the receding tide, right below
Portmeirion's windows. The Donald Halls,[1] alerted by a barking
dog, had spotted and identified her and immediately telephoned
me and the Marine Biology Station at Bangor, which at once
dispatched a jeepful of boffins, armed with winch, sledge and
grappling irons to secure the great fish for immediate dispatch in
a formalin-soaked shroud, to the Natural History Museum at
South Kensington, for post-mortem examination and report.
No other specimen of the species had ever been found anywhere
in or near British waters before—its normal habitat being the
Indian Ocean.

Unlike the Sturgeon, which by a statute of Edward III is a
royal fish, and if and when found is forfeit to the Crown, the
Tunny was deemed to be my personal property, I being the
riparian land-owner—whereby I earned a most handsome sort
of certificate as a Benefactor of the 'BRITISH MUSEUM
(NATURAL HISTORY)' and never, surely, was 'Honourable
Mention' gained so cheaply! No good reason could be advanced
by the authorities for the creature straying so far off course,
except that it might have picked up some congenial current that
ultimately wafted it into our own Tremadoc Bay which, being
shallow, warms up most commendably in response to sunshine
whence, we have always assumed, the luxuriance of the Port-

---

[1] Donald Hall, poet and writer, and Isabel Hall, artist, live in the home built
by the Author on the Portmeirion peninsula.

meirion peninsula's sub-tropical flora. Any 'ordinarily-extra-ordinary' fish should, of course, have properly been hung up stuffed in the bar of the Hotel—as was the celebrated 'Chavender or Chub'. But at six feet long it is better employed publicizing Portmeirion's enviable climate to frost-bitten Londoners in the Captain Cook section of the Natural History Museum. Instead of her bodily presence, long laments on the passing of beauty, by two accomplished poets, hang on the wall 'In Loving Memory'.

There has never been any need for direct advertising, as more than enough is done for us all for nothing by a seemingly endless series of mostly well-informed and well-illustrated articles by successive 'discoverers' as well as by its use as a 'set' for film and television. Parallel with the growth of Portmeirion's repute, and that of the place itself, has been the increased interest displayed by the English and Welsh Tourist Boards, who not only channel V.I.P. foreign visitors our way but also have generously subsidised various extensions and improvements deemed desirable.

Now Portmeirion, having celebrated its fiftieth birthday in 1976 with suitable gaiety and ebullience, has in a curious and most gratifying way taken over from me to stand in my place as I myself recede into the friendly shade of the middle nineties. No longer a dictator, I remain as a counsellor and critic whilst the now largely autonomous administration set up by my son-in-law Euan Cooper-Willis who, with his wife, my daughter Susan (both of the now flourishing Portmeirion Pottery at Stoke) masterminds the whole now quite considerable complex.

A charitable Trust was formed quite a while ago, and now owns the place so that it is, I hope, secure from the ravages of taxation which might otherwise have forced my descendants to sell part or all of it. Its future is further secured by the Department of the Environment which has scheduled the whole place as of 'Architectural and Historic Importance'. As a result, no-one can, now or ever, meddle with it in any way without official authority, not lightly given. At this moment of writing (Summer 1977) both its present and future prospects look to me, at least, as bright as is possible in a world that seems to be in the process

G. *Livingstone Evans, 15 Church Street, Blaenau Ffestiniog*

Plate 7 A cartoon by Hans Feibusch R.A. in the Dome at Portmeirion

THE NEW ARRIVAL

Place—Limbo   *Year—19??*

(Sir Christopher Wren, Sir Nicholss Hawksmoor and Sir John Vanbrugh are quizzing the latest arrival, Sir Clough Williams-Ellis.)

WREN: He says that he reveres our works and shares our principles and so claims that he too should be counted an Architect—in spite of his aberrations. How say you both?

HAWKSMOOR: (Dubiously) . . . Well . . .

VANBRUGH: (Dubiously) . . . Um . . .

Terence Spencer (I think!), and used in 'People'

Plate 8 The author and Lady Williams-Ellis at the Portmeirion Golden Jubilee
Carnival in 1976

of turning upside-down. No doubt Portmeirion will have, to some extent, to follow its tricky example, but it is fortunately a pretty adaptable organism and I have myself complete confidence in its happy survival far into the unforeseeable future.

H

14

Diversions and Diamonds

Prince Charles's Investiture as Prince of Wales on 1 July 1969 was the start of a series of festivities, some personal, some national, which have enlivened recent years. Amabel and I set out for Caernarfon Castle, bright and early in our utmost formal splendour, in obedience to the Earl Marshal's directive, and took our allotted places punctually, just behind the royal dais. The weather being fair, everything went with clockwork precision in accordance with its long, elaborate and much rehearsed sequence. Nothing whatever happened to relieve the monotony of inevitable waits between the successive set-pieces of ceremonial; the marshalling of the various processions, the arrival of the high dignitaries, the interspersed fanfares of trumpeters, blare of bands, choir singing and the culminating Investiture itself. What more, then, could one ask for? Well, a quickened tempo, a less rigidly regimented procedure, more garden-party freedom to wander and greet one's friends, before being confined to one's seat, more loud and livelier music, shorter set speeches, not all perhaps in both Welsh and English.

All the same, it was certainly a brilliantly produced spectacular, and if contrived more for the benefit of millions of T.V. viewers around the world than for that of us relatively few who saw it all 'live'—one is really ungenerous to criticise at all. All the same, had a few unscheduled incidents been given the chance of happening, or even been (unofficially) contrived, such as a stray *Derby* dog running around and being vainly chivvied off the course by Heralds or Bards or whoever, all in their ceremonial finery—what a boon to the poor commentators who had nothing outside their pre-cooked scripts to report, nothing wherewith to fill in all the gaps of the pre-ordained happenings—and how cheering for us chair-bound spectators! But I know that is just wishful nonsense, for in the prevailing flap about 'security' everything had to be rigidly tightened up and scrutinized—even our luncheon basket and Amabel's handbag being rummaged through at the Castle entry, though we were not actually 'frisked'.

There was nothing like that at the last Investiture in 1911 (of which I was one of the very few survivors at this one)—a relatively free and easy affair. Anyway no-one challenged me when, finding my seat in the sun too blazingly hot (88° was recorded) I left it to climb the dominating Eagle Tower, where alone on its topmost turret, I enjoyed both a lovely breeze and a bird's-eye view of all the goings-on both within and without the Castle. Unthinkable this time, when I dare say my commanding vantage point was manned by some fully armed lynx-eyed security man with a machine gun. Elaborate traffic control had made car-parking easy, but nothing could expedite our escape homewards as we crept and halted for miles before getting anything like a clear run—well aware that we should be late for an ambassadorial and ministerial dinner party at Portmeirion to which the big-wigs would have beaten us through having privileged parking places and official cars and drivers.

Then followed the Investiture Ball at Glynllifon, I suppose the largest country house in Wales, that for years has been an agricultural college. Approaching it from a direction new to me and in the dark, we found ourselves in a tunnel that delivered us into a large gaunt unlighted courtyard that I had never seen before, with three tiers of blank windows staring down at us without a hint of welcome. Yet we knew we had come to the right place on the right night (ticket and security checks again at the gates because of Royalty) but where was the much-heralded Ball? Spying a little door that opened, we found ourselves in a sort of luggage room that led on through various offices into the hinder parts of the great house itself, at the far end of which we at last discovered the entry to a vast three-aisled marquee built out on the lawn around one of the old fountains. Slipping out into the garden, I at last beheld the main front that I remembered, not really very good Palladian but, skilfully floodlit, looking impressive enough, its pediment and columns standing out nobly against the shadows.

I don't know how many bands—military and string—or how many floor-shows or how many guests there were. But certainly it was by far the largest and noisiest party we had ever attended— yet agreeable because all were so clearly out to enjoy themselves and relax in celebration of the Investiture itself being safely and indeed triumphantly over. Still there were certainly too many of us and, as one lady rather snobbishly remarked, 'I have never in all my life attended such a terribly *inclusive* party.' Even leaving early as we did, it was not until between 3 and 4 a.m. that we got home to bed. I don't put this forward as a typical day off in my 87th year, but I do record that I remained next day entirely unaffected by this unaccustomed bout of assorted dissipations.

In the summer of 1973, Portmeirion decided that my ninetieth birthday would be a good enough pretext for one of its celebrations—a beano, a fiesta—which it likes to mount every so often, and is really pretty good at. It was certainly a very generous, not to say formidable affair, starting after Saturday lunch and fizzing on until after midnight with the most prodigal fireworks display ever seen or imagined by any of the cheering company, one of whom—a distinguished and most popular painter—being so moved by it all that he obligingly fell into a fountain pool to everyone's delight, as aptly expressing their own feelings of reckless exaltation. But it all began with a long-running afternoon tea party for local friends, tenants, employees and the rest, in and around a marquee, whilst a full band blared melodiously away under the Bristol Colonnade, until a move to

the central Piazza was signalled for the formal ceremony—
which was the unveiling of a monumental lion by my neighbour
Lord Harlech who, in his characteristically generous speech,
welcomed the whole Portmeirion set-up as a 'Good Thing', for
all that it dominates his view across the estuary from his own
ancestral manor house.

He and I (who followed him) were formally introduced in both
Welsh and English by Wynford Vaughan Thomas, who was known
to all as broadcaster and by his Presidency of the Council for the
Protection of Rural Wales, with which I have been closely
associated from its first foundation. The pedestal of the lion—
which is thought to be a seventeenth-century creature—bears the
inscription:

Presented to Portmeirion and its Founder,
Sir Clough Williams-Ellis, by his friends and colleagues
on his 90th birthday, May 28th 1973.

There had been a morning party in the Pantheon (the dome)
mostly for architects, and a tour of mine around the place in a
beflowered and decorated pony-trap driven by my then horse-
orientated granddaughter, Menna. Later followed dinner for some
200 friends, both those from a distance, London and abroad, who
were staying the weekend, and such welcome neighbours as were
within reach. After dinner—a general move to the Hercules
Hall for the ball, where more speeches were demanded from
Sir Donald Gibson and myself, two fresh bands (one 'steel' and
most exhilarating) having arrived, and finally, those culminating
fireworks. Mercifully the weather was kind (the whole affair
must have been a sadly damp squib if it had *not* been); all the
elaborate arrangements worked to a miracle (to my surprise), the
only sadness being that Amabel only lately out of hospital, was
not fit to join in it all.

Finding myself jammed at the entry to the ballroom alongside
Jeremy Thorpe and his glamorous and famously musical bride,[1] I
remarked: 'We are bidden by the Queen to a Menuhin concert
and a dinner party at Windsor—Amabel isn't fit to go. I am a

[1] It was following the consecration of the memorial monument that I had
designed to his first wife, tragically killed in a car accident, that my mis-
adventure with the Archbishop's baggage, described on p. 49, took place.

musical ignoramus and if it's for connoisseurs I shall probably know none of them. Anyway it will be a devil of a journey getting there and back, right on top of all *this*, so I'm refusing.' 'No, you are NOT,' they said, 'because we're going to take you with us—we'll pick up wherever you are staying in London, whenever you say—run you down to Windsor and back again.' And so—providentially—it was; I was picked up at the Athenaeum and duly delivered back there in the small hours. I in fact found any number of friends and old acquaintances at the party, and of course the Thorpes seemed to know most of the rest— political and musical especially—Marion, as formerly Lady Harewood, having of course been long court-conditioned.

Arrived at the head of Windsor Castle's great staircase before entering 'The Presence', a Court official came up to me with 'Sir Clough, the Queen wishes you to dine after the concert at her own table. You will find it a round one, about half-way up the gallery, laid for eight and decorated with roses. You will be seated between the Duchess of Grafton and Dame Freya Stark.' After a gulp of surprise, I found myself entirely unalarmed—the other table guests being Menuhin himself on the Queen's right, as very properly her guest of honour, whom I had never met before, and a new minister and his wife.

Her Majesty was not in the least 'majestic' but relaxed and gay and apparently enjoying the admirable dinner as much as any of us, being clearly very well amused by her Guest of Honour. Dinner over, the Queen stood up, flanked by her uniformed attendants who had stood on either hand behind her chair, the whole company of other diners also standing up to attention—the Queen herself proceeding to the cleared length of the gallery ahead of the general exit. A whisper in my ear by some other Court Official in (what is it?—the 'Windsor Uniform'?): 'She hates parading alone—go and join her!'

Well, that *was* a bit alarming—but nothing for it but obedience, so there I was—sole escort under the doubtless astonished scrutiny of a hundred, two hundred, I don't know how many pairs of eyes—but the Queen herself entirely unconcerned and easy, responding most amiably to whatever feeble conversation gambits I contrived to launch. I had clean forgotten that it is *not* for the subject to raise topics with the monarch, and that one should preface or end anything one might be called upon to say with 'Your Majesty' or 'Ma'am'. My gaucherie did not seem to be noticed, but whoever it may be who arranges royal occasions may I think have a little note against my name 'not palace trained'.

The same easy cordiality prevailed when, later, I accompanied her round the library where she picked out books and special exhibits, some of which she herself seemed to think as of somewhat dubious authenticity. Prince Philip took me on a brief architectural tour to show me various improvements that the Queen and he had made—mostly for added convenience which had clearly been badly needed. He had, in fact, been alerted by the Queen on my presentation, when she turned to him with: 'Philip, you surely know Sir Clough, don't you?' His response being: 'But of course—architect, Cornwall, and all that.' Or that is what I *heard*, and thought 'your geography of the U.K. needs brushing up—*my* habitat is Snowdonia, and is where we first met.' But it emerged that he had just been visiting and apparently much admiring Cornwell, in Oxfordshire, referred to in Chapter Two, where I had been let loose for some years between the wars, and it was that that launched us so aptly on our architectural tour.

The Queen Mother claimed to remember our meeting up in the mist at Pen-y-Gwryd, where I had been commanded to explain and display the extent and intention of the proposed Snowdonia National Park to King George VI and herself, at that time supposed to be 'top secret'. And indeed so it would have remained, even from the Monarch himself, had I not demanded and got a large raised map sent down from the Ministry concerned, against just such an unlucky weather hazard. It was all we had to look at as visibility was down to some fifty yards. Polite interest was, of course, expressed but the whole thing must have been intolerably boring to the Royals who had had a long drive carefully planned to display the splendours of the area—entirely blotted out by low cloud, mist and drizzle. The whole matter of the exact location, extent and boundaries of our National Parks was still awaiting the seal of final government approval and was in the meantime 'top secret', as was officially and firmly impressed upon me. As I revealed all on my special raised map to the King, I wondered whether I ought to warn him—'I hope your Majesty will keep all this under your crown'—but in fact I didn't. After all, monarchs *are* different. But the Queen did ask a pretty shrewd question, that has not yet been satisfactorily answered; 'It's fine,' she said, 'preparing all this for the enjoyment of the people; but what is being done to prepare the people *for* such enjoyment?'

I have wandered away from my visit to Windsor and back a generation or so in time, without a word about the concert that was the centrepiece of the whole memorable party. Menuhin himself led his own orchestra of course brilliantly, and to my delight played the simpler compositions of the most august composers so that even I could be entranced as, obviously, were others as musically illiterate as myself. Tact, informality and friendliness indeed seemed to pervade the whole widely mixed but dazzling party, and I felt that there was still much to be said for so civilized a Monarchy, particularly when some other heads of state appear to be giving so little satisfaction to those who chose them.

The following year I received a letter out of the blue from Lord Butler, Master of my old College, Trinity, saying that he had been asked to invite me to its forthcoming 'Feast'. Knowing nothing whatever about such celebrations—having gone down after only three terms, and of course without a degree, and having had no contact at all with the place since—I nonetheless accepted, out of flattered curiosity. Then arrived the programme and necessary directives, with the list of honoured guests, including William Whitelaw whom I had expected to find a broken man after his Irish experiences, but who radiated robust good-humour and made an extremely amusing speech. I could only account for my own presence in so prestigious a gathering on the score of my absurd antiquity—probably the only Freshman of as long ago as 1900 still surviving.

Full evening dress with Orders and Decorations was ordained, and what with the Master in his Garter Insignia, and the colourful academic robes generally, we certainly made a pretty festive-looking lot. We were received in the great Drawing Room of the

Master's Lodge, which I well remembered from dining with the then Master, Dr. Montague Butler, Lord Butler's kinsman, over seventy years before, as described in my earlier autobiography. There were ladies present whom we however abandoned when we ourselves entered the Hall for our Feast. And Feast indeed it was, Grace most sweetly sung by Chapel choristers, a dinner of quite outstanding excellence with wines to match, and a pervading gala atmosphere, rare indeed at any formal or ritual gathering. Our move to the Combination Room for dessert, liqueurs, coffee and so on seemed to enhance rather than diminish the general bonhomie—one exchanged neighbours and was better able to follow the conversational leads of the Master, still presiding at the head of a long polished table, reflecting the candle-light and its load of college plate, fruit and all other possible edible trimmings. First to last, the lavishness of the whole occsion was astonishing against the contemporary background of limited service and restricted menus.

I suppose that past benefactions and endowments have provided ample funds specifically earmarked for the cosseting of the college Fellows, as a second non-gala high-table dinner at Trinity was only marginally less lavish; which also went for a dinner with Dr. Joseph Needham,[1] Master of Caius, *the* authority on Chinese art and history. Though my invitation had been for the Feast and one night's stay only, a providential week-end rail-strike made escape impossible, so that I enjoyed three nights hospitality at the commodious Judge's Lodgings next to the Master's Lodge in the Great Court, Cambridge having just ceased to be an Assize Town.

An old friend, Sir Leslie Martin, on the point of retiring from his architectural professorship, carried me off to lunch at his furiously picturesque old mill-house at Shelford, and thereafter on a tour of most of the buildings that had so changed the face of the Cambridge I had known and loved, over two generations ago. Despite the great expertise, enthusiasm and geniality of my host, I found it difficult to appreciate, let alone like, much of what I was shown and only really felt happy in my guide's

[1] J. Needham, F.R.S., Author of the multi-volume and still-appearing *A History of Chinese Science and Technology*.

own home where, like most modernist architects, he was en-capsuled in the gracious artifacts of long ago.

Next day—Sunday—was as different as could be, as Dr. Lu[1]—Dr. Needham's Chinese colleague—volunteered to drive me to Ely, which I had not seen since bicycling out to admire it under snow, just seventy-three years before. On this return visit I felt the whole great cathedral somehow more sinister and indeed threatening than uplifting, seeming to express temporal power and superstition rather than Christian love and charity. I saw it as a great mediaeval fortress of a quasi Prince-Bishop, built to overawe and subjugate the poor peasants of its surround-ing fen-country, as well as to compete with and outclass less ostentatious dioceses. Wherein I may be completely in error. But being in general an admirer of great mediaeval buildings—I do confess that I found Ely intimidating rather than uplifting, and definitely a diminisher of my own never very robust Christian faith.

The amenities of the minute town of Ely are, apart from its ecclesiastical buildings, definitely minimal—with just one sur-prising exception. That was a quite admirable Chinese restaurant, known of course to Dr. Lu. There, consulting the management in their and her own native tongue, she ordered and it produced so admirable a meal as to give me quite a new respect for Chinese cooking and—incidentally—a less critical assessment of the great cathedral.

After the Cambridge party, there was something of a lull in my 'fun and games' department, relieved only by the Athenaeum's prestigious celebration of the 150th anniversary of its foundation, presided over with the greatest verve by Prince Philip, and a surprisingly lively get-together it turned out to be. I had become the 'father' of the place, both by virtue of age and the date of my election, 1918, and the congratulatory telegram from the club's chairman and committee did, I admit, make me feel truly venerable.

My next party, far from involving a journey to London that becomes steadily more tedious, was right here where I am now writing, at my ancestral Snowdonian home, Plas Brondanw.

[1] Lu Gwei-Djen, co-author of *A History of Chinese Science and Technology*.

Amabel and myself and some four hundred friends celebrated in 1975, the sixtieth anniversary of our wedding, our *Diamond* wedding day, which we hold is quite something even nowadays. The text of the illustrated invitation began thus:

> Sir Clough and Lady Williams-Ellis greatly hope
> that..............................may be free to join them in
> celebrating their Diamond Wedding at Plas Brondanw,
> on Thursday, July 31st 1975 where, precisely 60 years
> before to the day, they were so cordially welcomed home
> by their neighbours after their very early morning wedding
> in Surrey.

It was responded to, considerably beyond our hopes or expectations, but fortunately not at all beyond the ample provisions made, chiefly by the Portmeirion management and staff who mount such events with the greatest expertise and apparent enjoyment. A fine afternoon, a band and a harp and a constantly replenished buffet kept our guests good and happy. Friends we hadn't seen for years turned up from far and near, even from abroad, though the New Zealand contingent scarcely counted as 'guests' as they were two generations of our own descendants.

All the estate and village tenants were of course invited, many the children of those who had originally welcomed us so musically, and some who had sung on that occasion as little children, when we had arrived home on the evening of our wedding, away in an isolated little pilgrim church on a Surrey hilltop to which there was no approach except on foot, St. Martha's Chapel. Incidentally, my two daughters and their husbands had both by then been married for thirty years, so between them the two couples could just equal our own period of marriage.

15

The Author's Credo

(My Positively Final Appearance)

In the books I have written for the last fifteen years I have ended with last words intended as a final farewell to that indulgent public which has so kindly welcomed both my buildings and my books. I must therefore accept that the genuine finality of even the last words which I am about to write will be greeted with a certain scepticism. However, my age and infirmity convince me that this really will be my last publication and that in a final summing up of my activities I should be permitted to proclaim my artistic credo.

I hold that man's one special and unique part in the world is a spiritual and not a material one. Unless he believes that and (broadly) *acts* on that belief, constantly checking his actions against his own conscience and the best current thought on such difficult abstractions as—truth and beauty—he's not playing his proper part—he is letting the poor old world down—which indeed, in that case, might be better off without him. In a *nut-shell*: Sensibility is more important than mere Sense, and may even have a higher survival value. In his book *Art and Technics*, Lewis Mumford personifies these two great human aptitudes (Art and Technics) as, respectively, *Orpheus* and *Prometheus*—suggesting that it was the poetic music-maker rather than the practical fire-bearer who was the great civilizer, in that it was *he, Orpheus*, who enabled us (by means of symbols) to express fellowship and love. I, too, would stress the civilising mission of the poet—the artist—as even above that of the also necessary, also admirable, more popular, more practical, plumber. He and his like (the clever technicians of every sort) may contrive to *keep* us alive, and to provide us with all kinds of practical ingenuities and amenities to that end—which is fine—BUT—but what's the good of it all, unless we are also GLAD we are alive—which isn't nearly as widespread a condition as it should surely be.

Orpheus has been crowded out by Prometheus. The poet, the artist, is ousted by the practical plumber. Beauty has too often been made to give way to, and been sacrificed to, other things. For instance, we in Snowdonia are continually alarmed by threats of widespread and devastating hydro-electric development. To be even asked to give up (and for ever) something so rare and precious as the fortunate integrity of Snowdonia, in order (and quite doubtfully) to relieve a technical peak-load embarrassment in the Midlands, that is most certainly only temporary, is surely dis-quieting in the topsy-turvy values it suggests, and not a little shocking—as if asking us to be cordially co-operative in arranging for our mother's electrocution and then for the disposal of her mutilated body! We must refuse to be accessories! As between the power or the glory, I believe that most of those same Midlanders in whose name this horrid thing is proposed would, for their own sake as well as for ours, be overwhelmingly against the rape of Snowdonia, as thousands have indeed loyally testified, feeling (and rightly) that its loveliness was their own heritage as much as ours. The utilitarian electrifiers claim that it's only SENSE to ensure our waterfall's 'Full Employment'—as 'realistic' as, say, providing treadmills for otherwise unproductive ballerinas!—a project only hindered by our tiresome *un*realistic,

Welsh sensibility, that actually puts the work of God above those of the Engineer.

I have devoted much of my working life to resisting those who base on some fantastic perversion of commercial arithmetic their 'modest proposals' to destroy the environment, our common heritage. It has encouraged me to see how, in recent years, the support has grown for a repudiation of the purely materialistic approach. The suspicion has begun to spread, that when you sell your soul to the Devil for short term gain, it always turns out a very one-sided bargain.

I don't for a moment believe that anyone commits the horrors I have in mind just out of diabolical glee, or because they themselves *enjoy* the squalid results, because alas! it is tragically clear that, mostly, they haven't yet learnt really to enjoy anything at all that needs a little sensitive understanding—which is tragic for them, seeing what they must miss in life in 'eye-pleasure'— and a danger to the rest of us. And they are the overwhelming majority, these poor, numb, half-alive folk—too used to ugliness to protest, too ill-taught to know better, and the untaught are the fault of the unteaching. Somehow we must replace that cruelly maiming vacuum—that lack of perception and civility—by its opposite, if we are ever to become—and LOOK LIKE—a decently civilized land—or be a sanely HAPPY one.

But these are only the victims, more planned against than planning. The real trouble is that those who should be on the side of the angels, the leaders of the architectural profession, are all too often as blind and insensitive in their work as any laymen. As I once said in a discussion on the question: 'Is Architecture sick, and should it be reviewed?'—'Architecture sick! What an optimistic diagnosis! Sick! Why, it's been *dead* these thirty years—a "STIFF" if ever there was one!' That was my instinctive reaction, no doubt a pretty silly one, but then remember my age group—that my years of practice had handsomely overlapped those of Norman Shaw and Philip Webb, with Lutyens as my guiding star, so that being 'with it' is quite beyond me—when 'IT' is modern architecture—or indeed current sculpture, painting or music. The typical reaction, you will say, of an old square still imagining himself a golden section rectangle! 'Should it be revived?' Could it be? Depends on what we mean by 'it', as so memorably emphasized by Alice in 'Wonderland'. Can one, in fact, revive a corpse? As to that, I recall a former President of the R.I.B.A., Hal Goodhart-Rendel, of course, discussing the propriety of architects putting their names on all their buildings, saying 'Of course they are reluctant—you might just as well expect murderers to sign their corpses.'

Starting from where we are now (as we must) what are the steps towards health and salvation? Whence can come the kiss of Life? If my so impressively capable successors could only descend from their CLINICAL and NEGATIVE abstractions to the level of warm humanity—could build with more loving-kindness—could bring back delight to rejoin the firmness and commodity wherein they (sometimes) so excel—then we would surely be on our way to something better—something pleasurable. I confess myself just *bored* by most modern buildings, positively irritated by many, because they seem to have so wantonly thrown away obvious chances of interest and distinction—to have wilfully withheld opportunities for delight—for imaginative, sensitive detailing and for the appreciation of arts, skills and craftsman-ship as well as overall harmony. Many of these skills are dying or have already died for lack of patronage.

Even the over-elaborate and under-bred buildings that were the common currency of my youth did at least hold a certain interest, melancholy and cautionary as it might be. There was plenty to look at, God wot, even if only to deplore. THEY emphatically were *not* negative—too many, indeed, excruciat-ingly positive, clamouring raucously for notice. God forbid we should return to anything like that, which indeed I take it is what we are reacting *from*. But don't let us go on reacting so aridly, so drearily, so emptily—let us dare to be a little more friendly—even a little gay. Let us use our wings. There was a glimmer of hope in 1951—The Festival of Britain Year—where is it now? If a heretic deviationist such as I were allowed to offer up a prayer on behalf of British Architecture, it would be 'GOD, GRANT GRACE'.

Certainly one impoverishment of our time is the steep decline of craftsmanship, in many branches to the very verge of total disappearance, with no present sign or promise of survival. This impoverishment is, of course, partly the result of new techniques, the availability of hitherto unknown materials and of mass production—but it is difficult to decide whether it is primarily the lack of demand or the drying up of the supply that is chiefly responsible for our present deprivation of individual inventiveness and skilful execution. No scope or chance for any such display of talent is given by the property developers and bureaucrats now responsible for so much of the country's building, and precious little in the bleak university and other supposedly cultural orientated establishments, where one might have expected some gesture towards the hand-crafts, and the emphasizing of whatever structural impact a building may be intended to convey by the apt introduction of occasional highlights of interest that could leaven the whole lump and enable it to make some sort of contact with humanity.

As it is, nearly all our most eminent architects, responsible for our largest and most prestigious structures, seem to have forgotten that these are to serve the natural needs of soft little animals— us—not machines. Until they come to think differently and bring back 'Delight' to rejoin 'Firmness' and 'Commodity' to complete the trinity essential to a real and valid architecture—we shall continue to be deprived of any fresh addition to our existing muster of beautiful old buildings, which is itself being steadily eroded and reduced.

But now at last I seem to be no longer alone in my disenchantment, but supported in my revolt by various eminences who, too, appear to be on the recoil from continued submission to dehumanised technology. I think there will soon be more; even the technical press being now apparently in the throes of an agonising re-appraisement. In America, Lewis Mumford has long been with me. In France, Francois Spoerry with his Port Grimaud, and Peter Shepherd the late President of the R.I.B.A., as well as Eric Lyons the present one, are also taking a new look at the architectural status quo. I begin to feel that my own gloomy assessment is not just senile grumpiness. Even Lord Esher's important recent book *Parameters and Images* dealing brilliantly and in depth with the reaction between men and buildings

throughout history down to today, displays a philosophic confidence in the future that I should dearly like to share. Meanwhile
I stubbornly go along with Goodhart-Rendel: 'In buildings made
for the service of man, architecture begins where utilitarianism
leaves off, endowing practical contrivance with aesthetic significance.' I would also subscribe to Edwin Lutyens' aphorism:

Architecture with its love and passion begins where function is
achieved.

16

As of Now

So here I am at ninety-four. Life seems to rush past me now with ever-increasing acceleration so that it's Spring again before one has finished savouring the colours of Autumn. I don't complain, but it can be a little confusing, like the metric system or our new coinage, neither of which I have quite mastered. One's latter years are not proper years at all—they shrink and shrink like the Pound in our pockets.

Looking back, I certainly have to concede that, taken overall, my own allowance of good luck seems to have been quite unfairly generous throughout my whole life as compared with the normal ration and, well conscious of my advantage, I have tried—though far too rarely—to render some sort of service, public or private, in return for all that I have received. This persistent luck began with my birth and up-bringing, persisted throughout school, college and my professional career, and gave me a wife whose companionship over sixty years has been my greatest stroke of luck of all. Then nothing but irrational luck could have brought me through the First World War unscathed and settled us in the old Snowdonia home of my ancestors. Two highly talented daughters and their families add to our content, though (our one great sadness) our only son, who had gone straight from Cambridge into my own old regiment, the Welsh Guards, as soon as he reached the minimum required age, was soon killed in the storming of Monte Cassino in the Second World War.

Besides the essentials of good luck and good health, I have, I suppose, one further quality which has contributed to making my life a happy and satisfactory one, and that quality is single-mindedness. As I have recounted, I have never seriously wavered from my passionately loved profession of architecture, landscape and design. It is perhaps not mere capriciousness that my memory works as it does. Whilst I can almost always recall the details of any building or landscape with almost photographic accuracy, the features of the human countenance scarcely register at all, and I am perfectly capable of returning the friendly smiles and greetings of someone I had dined with only the evening before with a blank stare, his (or her) name having vanished away as completely as their visible identities. This extreme lack of facial memory of course showed up most glaringly when I was in the army where, because of it, I could never have made a good regimental officer—one young man in uniform being quite indistinguishable from another. Even in civil life, I have no doubt lost innumerable potential friends through looking straight through them without a nod of recognition or even a non-committal 'Hello!'

The truth is that for me it is a very exceptional human being whose character or appearance is as vivid and real to me as that of countless buildings. With this fundamental bias, I have never found the least difficulty in devoting myself to architecture, landscape and design. Indeed I find it hard to imagine how I could possibly exist for even a few months if I were entirely cut off from my work. To me personally it seems that capital punishment would be a far less dreadful penalty than a year in prison. I have always felt that the depressing thing about Heaven is that it is supposed to be perfect, and so leaves no scope for me to improve upon its appearance!

Even now my work goes on. I am engaged on various literary

ploys, which have ever been my secondary life-line. I am always delighted to design tombstones or monuments for my old friends, and of course there is always Portmeirion. Although, as I have said, Portmeirion is basically completed, there remain continual small improvements called for by changing circumstances, or suggested as I walk around. For the rest, I have in my leisured old age the time to read. Though I can no longer read the print of ordinary books, there are the special large-type editions of many that are provided free by the County Libraries, and at times I relax with one of the wide and excellent range of 'Talking Books' provided by the British Talking Book Service, while radio and television have largely banished solitude.

As I have perhaps indicated, human relationships, except those of my nearest and dearest or very particular friends, make less difference to me than they do to many; I am generally of a buoyant disposition and with no talent for introspection or self-analysis I cheerfully accept that I am probably considered less matey than I might be. Quite apart from any human companionship, I have a gay and devoted shadow in the shape of an elegant little Papillon bitch who follows me about all around the house and gardens, and constantly challenges me to ball-games in the forecourt, dancing on her hind-legs to demand attention. She sleeps at the foot of my bed and if she thinks I am sitting up too late, trots upstairs and settles down ahead of me, not to stir until we are both called for breakfast.

Until 'Suki' arrived as a Diamond Wedding present from our daughter Susan, I had no idea how generally stimulating the presence of a jolly little animal could be. I am very well aware that Suki and I have the rare luck to enjoy a setting that suits us both to perfection—but wherever conditions are favourable, I do most strongly commend the very old thus to link up with the exuberant vitality of a fellow-creature without—so it would seem—a care in the world. For some, small children may supply this therapy—'grand', 'great-grand' or other, but I have none such now young enough and anyhow the responsibility may inhibit. In any case I am not completely at ease with the young of my own species.

I suppose that I seem to outsiders to have attained a Plateau of

Serenity because I can still do most of the things I really care about, largely because I have followed my own exhortations to *be oneself, presume failure so as to be happily surprised by relative success* and *follow your bent*—few and meagre signposts I know, to anyone bound in that direction, but of surprising efficacy.

Moreover my memory, so doubtful and misleading about present social engagements and the like, retains so accurate a store of the views and buildings which I have seen in my life that I have no need to revisit Venice or Portofino to see in my mind's eye the prospects which I may happen to require. There is nothing, nor ever has been in war or peace, to keep me from *dreaming* and even, now and again, from actually drawing what I dream. If nothing else, there are always the possible if improbable extensions, alterations or adornments both for Portmeirion and for my own old home to be mulled over, developed and, more often than not, getting no further than that. In short, what with intermittent trips abroad and more than enough selected human contacts and social occasions, few, if any, chinks or crannies are left for boredom, which for as long as I can remember I have always been aware of as a menacing and minatory little black speck, just perceptible over the horizon, that might yet, given half a chance, expand into a monstrous great black cloud of overwhelming boredom, until death do us part.

Even if some may call my 'Plateau' the 'Shelf', I look forward to the rest of my sojourn there without the least misgiving, but with the liveliest interest, for might it not turn out that I or one of my fellows was to become the first of Shaw's ancients, as described in his play *Back to Methuselah*, who had at last broken through the prevailing age-barrier and grown-up above and beyond the pitifully puerile notions of our nominal three-score-years-and-ten life span, that has never yet given any race or people sufficient time really to develop their full mental potentialities.

Failing such an admittedly unlikely happening, there is still the bright hope that our new Archbishop of Canterbury, Dr Donald Coggan, has so valiantly dared to hold out to us, that of euthanasia being not only merciful to distressful and obviously terminal sufferers, but that it would release our hard-pressed doctors and hospitals for the better service of those who still sorely need more medical care than has ever yet been available. Under the influence of Francis Galton, I myself long ago joined his 'Eugenic Society' and signed-on for euthanasia—prompted a little perhaps by one of the commandments of my kinsman's[1] rhymed and ironic decalogue:

> Thou shalt not kill but need not strive
> Officiously to keep alive.

Even plateaux have their boundaries and I found one of them when only last year my old friend and neighbour, Lord Anglesey, insisted that I must give the opening address at the ceremonial handing over of the whole of his splendid home of Plas Newydd to the National Trust—another old and valued friend.

I had long been cutting down speaking engagements of any kind—a departure from an activity stretching back to my seminal visit to that old town planning magician, Professor Sir Patrick Geddes, in his Edinburgh outlook tower; a visit that, in my early twenties, launched me on my almost life-long ploy of lecturing and speech-making on the general themes of town and country planning, conservation, architecture and so forth. That snow-balled into almost a career that gradually absorbed more and more of my time and energy for nearly two generations. I addressed almost every type of audience, from all the major public schools to civic societies and the like both at home and overseas.

I had announced that the scarcely-to-be-avoided response to my ninetieth birthday celebrations at Portmeirion was to be the last speech of my life. And so it was, until Henry Anglesey hauled me out of retirement. In vain I pleaded the infirmity of age, that my memory would never hold what I might intend to say, that I was too blind to read any reminding notes and that anyhow I was being entertained to dinner that evening at Portmeirion by the President and Council of the Royal Institute of British Architects who would inevitably expect a speech of some sort from me in return for their felicitations; altogether too much for an old by-gone such as I. But Henry Anglesey, as resourceful as he is resolute, brushed my feeble pleadings aside with, 'But that's

---

[1] Arthur Hugh Clough

splendid! I will invite all the forty of your Portmeirion party to join in the celebrations here, so that by dinner time back at Portmeirion they will be too exhausted to want speeches from you or anyone else.'

But he had underestimated the stamina of sight-seeing architects and that evening I was duly called upon to speak. I obediently arose and said, 'I am sorry, but this afternoon, the hottest recorded July day for over two hundred and fifty years, I made the very last speech of my life, not without difficulty. So never again. BUT, if you will regard me as, say, a caged hyena that it might be amusing to provoke by poking it with rude questions, professional or otherwise, I shall enjoy snarling my responses.' And so it was and we had one of the liveliest after dinner set-to's that I can recall.

My little afternoon speech at Plas Newydd (over which I had agonised so absurdly) amounted, according to the records, to no more than this:

My Lords, Ladies and Gentlemen—on behalf of Lord and Lady Anglesey, Plas Newydd and the National Trust—Welcome!

Welcome to all, and not only to you, right here today, but to generations yet to follow you, who will, I hope, share in our own delight in landscape, architecture, painting and history, and in the elegant lifestyle of our more fortunate predecessors.

Most happily our co-host, Henry Anglesey, himself goes with the home of his ancestors, or rather *stays* with it in a reserved corner, as the ideal custodian and director or whatever. Quite apart from his intimate knowledge of the whole splendid set-up and its historic relics, he shines in his own right as a distinguished military historian— ranging far beyond the exploits of his famous great- great- grandfather, elevated to a marquisate for his part in our great victory at Waterloo as Wellington's Leader of Cavalry and Second in Command.

Just reflect! But for the personal gallantry and military expertise of those two leaders, that 'damned close run thing', as they called it, might well have gone the other way, and I should now be addressing you in bastard French and the victorious Emperor would be watching us from atop that column there in place of our host's great ancestor!

As to the rest of this enchanted place—what a matchless setting! What an appropriate architectural response! Where the famous architect James Wyatt responded by shedding his usual strict classical style and went all romantic and Gothic. Purists may regret his being so carried away, but I can well understand his being so influenced by the fairy-land magic of the setting—vastly enhanced since his day by the gardening knowledge and zeal of our so generous host and benefactor.

The place is full of military and historic records—including the very first articulated artificial leg, made for the gallant first Marquis when his own was carried away by a cannon ball.

Wellington's remark, 'You have lost a leg.'—His laconic response, 'By God, so I have!'

They remained close friends into ripe old age, and I recall someone's moving description of them hobbling arm in arm up the central aisle of the Great Exhibition of 1851 to pay their respects to their young Queen—Victoria.

But back to Plas Newydd itself, where to me and to many others Rex Whistler's inspired murals that adorn the State Dining Room are its crowning glory. I had always thought that they should be in some way 'nationalised'— and now, most happily, they *are*. Alas! they are too his chief memorial, as he was killed, still in his splendid youth, fighting most gallantly in Hitler's War in my own old regiment—the Welsh Guards.

And that's all—except perhaps to explain why on earth this honourable office of, as it were, 'opening' Plas Newydd was planted on *me* of all people—who will be a hundred years old in next to no time. And that's apparently *why*—because, it seems, I was the oldest discoverable member of the National Trust and friend of the donor's family who could still stand up on its hindlegs and say a croaking 'Bow Wow'.

Epilogue

Here Endeth

As, by the time I might have qualified for a brief paragraph in the obituary columns in the daily press, our shrinking newspapers will probably have abandoned the amiable practice of celebrating deaths, save those of the undisputedly eminent, it has occurred to me that I might well plug the foreseen gap with the sort of stuff that a well-informed yet friendly correspondent could well have written for the stand-by files of—say—'The Guardian' or 'The Times', as I myself have on occasion done. I assume that he would have been instructed to restrict his commentary to my professional career and not to waste space on my chequered private life, my family, or anything even marginally irrelevant to his brief.

Abstract: Quite naturally and inevitably, Sir Clough's sudden, precocious and precipitate, entirely unqualified youthful plunge into architectural practice was resented by the already established practitioners (none of whom he knew, nor they him) as being as unseemly an intrusion as would be an outsider impudently gate-crashing an intimate private party. As, however, he seemed to be increasingly accepted by the public and the media as a perfectly serious 'professional' and soon even welcomed as a rising new light on the then somewhat dim architectural horizon, he was eventually and most generously welcomed into the official fold. Amongst its established leaders, there was only one with whom he found himself in almost total and abiding accord, and that was Edwin Lutyens, who had always contrived to keep himself out of the professional fishpond, to the immeasurable loss of its less gifted occupants.

From modest beginnings, Sir Clough's clientele rapidly expanded until, by 1910 or so, he had quite a substantial practice, mostly concerned with country houses large and small, villages, landscaping, gardens and conservation. Though interrupted by two World Wars (his own the 1914–18) his practice seemed to have been invigorated by each, and his output of books, some in collaboration with his wife and others, on architecture and allied subjects, accelerated. When in his nineties his output dropped, it was less from lack of interest or capacity than simply because the existing economic climate was not such as to encourage enterprise, whether in building or publishing.

Chiefly owing to his almost total lack of formal architectural education, his detailed knowledge of classical and other phases of architecture was inexact and his dating no better, but he claimed that his library could always supply all that he lacked in such regards without cluttering up his mind with seldom needed minutiae. Though he respected scholarship and erudition, he held that unless joined to an intuitive and instinctive feeling for proportion, propriety, scale, setting, use and apt materials, they could produce none but Dead Sea fruits. This suggests a staunch belief in his own judgements, especially as regards scale, suitability to purpose, setting and environmental effect. It also implies a certain arrogance, for he admitted that he certainly felt his instincts were correct and infallible, given all the circumstances. He was concerned about texture and colour, though it was said of the latter that it became abnormal with advancing age.

He did not feel that he had been deeply influenced by anyone, except his mother, his wife and his old head master, Sanderson. But there were a number of people who did for a while redirect his thoughts, interests and outlook. The first of these was undoubtedly Sir Lawrence Weaver, whose biography indeed he ultimately wrote, under the promptings of Sir Stafford Cripps who held Weaver in similar affection and regard. Indeed for the last few years of Weaver's life, the three of them jointly ran a pottery at Ashstead for the benefit of disabled ex-servicemen, and although it prospered for a while, largely owing to Weaver's unique flair for publicity and salesmanship, it ultimately wilted and died, because, so it seemed, they had mistakenly tried to transplant an industry native to Staffordshire to alien Surrey soil, which is far from being clay. Among other people who influenced him were Sir Edwin Lutyens for architecture; Peter Thorpe for interest in social benefit ploys, and Claude Lovat-Fraser for colour sense; with Jan Morris for increased interest in words and literature generally. Generals Sir Hugh Ellis and Eliot Hotblack, both of the Royal Tank Corps, were certainly influential in sustaining his interest and morale throughout their War years together and beyond. Then there was Geoffrey Scott, and much earlier seminal contacts with Shaw and Wells.

So short a list suggests that books may have done more for him than he realized, though he maintained that he was, however unfortunately, nine-tenths just his own original self, though inevitably, if unconsciously, modified by a long and variegated life among all sorts and conditions of men and women, any meaningful contact with whom, however, seemed to him both rare and slight. There was just one exception to these sometimes relatively brief influences—or rather 'contacts'—his long and close association with Patrick Abercrombie who really did permanently change and widen his outlook.

He said he was not an expert on soil-engineering or foundations, structural stresses or drains, but always saw that *someone* was, and though he never sought insurance cover against architect's liability, in fact never had a claim of any sort made against him. He first made his mark with cheap rural and cottage and village work, but perhaps best expressed himself in his country houses for the cultivated well-to-do clients with whom he found it easy to establish cordial, co-operative relations. He would clearly have been a complete misfit in any big organisation concerned with large-scale property developments or industrial or other complex enterprises, being essentially a 'loner'— his own office, including pupils, never exceeding a dozen.

Though a member of a wide variety of Societies and Committees concerned with architecture, planning, the environment, conservation and so on, his chairmanships were always reluctant and his attendance irregular and minimal. Allergic as he was to committee work of any sort, he did nonetheless act as Chairman of the first of the New Towns— Stevenage—for its difficult initial period, but was probably more useful in all such situations as a writer and broadcaster than as an active, attentive and regular debater or director.

He accepted that insofar as he would be remembered, it would probably be because of his propagandist architectural demonstration at Portmeirion, but insisted that it really designed itself, he being merely a sort of medium through whom it contrived to bring itself to birth. More prosaically, he never drafted a general lay-out plan and left successive buildings to, as it were, design themselves according to their several functions, positions and settings, 'so as to join in harmonious ease with any earlier arrivals at the party—and their setting'. Though liking symmetry and formality, he also clearly enjoyed breaking both quite arbitrarily if dullness seemed to threaten. He thought that he always knew (again instinctively) when enough was enough. Not everyone was quite so sure.

Sticking honestly to his architectural brief, our imagined correspondent would refrain from any mention of my propensity for getting involved in libel actions and fruitless argle-bargles, or the fact that during my active war service abroad I was twice threatened with courts-martial for preferring my own ideas to those of G.H.Q.—but those little local difficulties were disposed of by my own General's report, promotion, dispatches and a decoration.

I am very well aware that a hostile biographer could make me out to have been an intolerable, interfering and irrepressible busy-body, quite inexplicably tolerated for the best part of a century by my long-suffering compatriots. It would no doubt be good for me to have my own necessarily rosier view of myself thus authoritatively counter-balanced, binocular vision being essential to any just assessment.

Meanwhile, *hic jacet*.

Index

Abercrombie, Sir Patrick, 127
Almost Perfect State, The, ix
Amalfi, 81–2
Anglesey, Marquis of, 122–3
Architect, The, 2
Architect Errant, 2, 26, 45
Arnold-Foster, Mrs., 39
Art and Technics, 113
Athenaeum, The, 71, 106, 110

Back to Methuselah, 121
Baker, Sir Herbert, 36
Baldwin, Stanley, 71–2
Battersea Pleasure Gardens, 13–14
Beazley, Elizabeth, 77
Bell, Lady, 76
Benda, Madame, 84
Bevan, Aneurin, 6
Bevin, Ernest, 2
Bishop Stortford College Memorial Hall, 53
Blackett, Patrick (Lord), 34, 64
Boston, Lord, 67
Boulestin, Marcel, 66
Brett, Christian (Viscountess Esher), 77
Brett, Lionel (Viscount Esher), 6, 77, 116
Brett-Young, Francis, 80
Brewer, Joseph, 57
British Talking Book Service, The, 120
Brownlow, Baron, 30–1
Butler, Andy, 36
Butler, Lord, 108
Butlin, Sir Billy, 67

Caernarfon Castle, 102
Calcutta, 37–8
Capri, 80–1
Carrara, 79
Caribbean, The, 26–32
Caserta, Palace of, Naples, 82

Casson, Sir Hugh, 11, 13, 37
Castle, Barbara, 19
Church, Richard, 36
Clough, Arthur Hugh, 122
Coggan, Dr. Donald (Archbishop of Canterbury), 121
Cooper-Willis, Euan, 100
Cooper-Willis, Menna, 105
Cooper-Willis, Susan, 100, 120
Cornwell, Oxfordshire, 5, 107; village street at, *plate 4b*
Corsica, 82–4
Council for the Protection of Rural Wales, 105
Country Life, 80
Crawford, Lord, 57
Cripps, Sir Stafford, 20, 126

Dalton Hall, Cumbria, 50–3, *plate 2b*; inspecting the roof timbers of, 51, *plate 3a*
de Hamel, Bruno, 20
Delano, Billy, 57
Delhi, 36
Douglas, Norman, 80

Elba, 78–9
Elmhirst, Leonard, 36
Elizabeth II (H.M. The Queen), 105–8
Elizabeth, The Queen Mother, 107
Ellis, General Sir Hugh, 127
Ely Cathedral, 110
Erice, 80
Etiquette, 76
Eugenic Society, The, 122

Family and Kinship in East London, 10–11
Feibusch, Hans, 6; cartoon by, *plate 7*
Festival of Britain, The, 3–4, 13–15, 115
Fiji, 32

Fitzwilliam, Lady, 72
French General Strike, 82–5

Galton, Francis, 122
Geddes, Professor Sir Patrick, 122
George VI, 107–8
Gibson, Sir Donald, 105
Glynllifon, 103
Goodhart-Rendel, Hal, 115, 117
Gowers, Sir Ernest, 9
Grafton, Duchess of, 106
Guardian, The, 125
Guards Club, The, 71

Haldane, J. B. S., 37
Hall, Donald, 99
Hall, Isabel, 99
Hambro, Jack, 32
Harlech, Lord, 105
Hatton Grange, Shropshire, temple at, *plate 1*
Herbert, Sir Alan, 58, 77
Hotblack, General Sir Eliot, 127

India, 36–8

Laughing Water, Kent, 53
Laughton, Charles, 60
Le Corbusier, 84
Littlehampton, 6
Llangoed Castle, Breconshire, 54–6, *plate 2a*
Lloyd George, memorials for, 48
Loch, Baron, 71
Lovat-Fraser, Claude, 127
Loved One, The, 59
Lu Gwei-Djen, Dr., 110
Lutyens, Sir Edwin, 36, 58, 71, 114, 117, 126, 127
Lyons, Eric, 116

Man and Superman, 65
Marquis, Don, ix
Marseilles, 84–5
Martin, Sir Leslie, 15, 109–10
Mathew, Sir Robert, 15, 17
Menuhin, Yehudi, 105–6
Mexico, 32–5
Monte Cassino, 119
Morris, Jan, 81, 127

Muffins, 65–6
Mumford, Lewis, 10, 11, 58, 87, 113, 116

Nantclwyd Hall, 45–7, *plate 3b*; bridge at, 46, *plate 4a*
Naples, 82
Napoleon, 77–8
National Parks, 21–5; dream about, 43–4
National Theatre, The, 17
National Trust, The, 7, 122–4
Natural History Museum, 99–100
Needham, Dr. Joseph, 109
Neel, Boyd, 59
Nehru, 36
Niven, David, 60
Noto, 80

Oronsay, The, 77–80; at Portofino, *plate 5a*

Parameters and Images, 116
Paris, 83
Pax Britannica, 81
Pen-y-Gwryd, 107
Percy, Lord Eustace, 72
Philip, Duke of Edinburgh, 107, 110
Plas Brondanw, 110, 119, 121
Plas Newydd, 122–4
Ponsonby, Sir John, 71
Port Grimaud, 88–94, *plate 5b*
Portmeirion, and Portofino, 79; and Capri, 81; and Port Grimaud, 93; grows up, 95–101; and Author's 90th birthday celebrations, 104–5, 120, 121, 127
Portofino, 79, 121, *plate 5a*
Prince of Wales, Investiture of, 102–3

Ramsey, Dr. Michael (former Archbishop of Canterbury), 49
Reilly, Sir Charles, 36
Reith, Lord, 9, 31
Rhiwlas, *plate 6a*
R.I.B.A. Council at Portmeirion, 122
Royal Festival Hall, 15–17
Russell, Bertrand (Lord), 38

St. Paul's Cathedral, 99
Sanderson, Frederick, 126

Savona, 79
Scott, Geoffrey, 127
Second World War, effect on Portmeirion, 96
Shaw, George Bernard, 65, 121, 127
Shaw, Norman, 114
Shepherd, Peter, 116
Sicily, 79–80
Silkin, Lord, 7, 9–10
Sim, Alistair, 63
Simon, André, 66
Simon, Lady, 11
Snowdonia National Park, 21–5, 107–8; and hydro-electric development, 113
South Wind, 80
Spoerry, François, and Port Grimaud, 88–93; and new town near Toulon, 93–4, 116
Stark, Dame Freya, 106
Stevenage New Town, 7–9, 127
'Stop-me-and-buy-one' temple, 48, *plate 1*
Stowe, 72
Strachey, Amabel, *see* Williams-Ellis, Amabel
Strachey, Rt. Hon. John, 37, 59
Suki, 120

Taj Mahal, 37
Thorpe, Rt. Hon. Jeremy, 105
Thorpe, Marion, 106
Thorpe, Peter, 127
Thunnus Albacarus, 99
Times, The, 125
Travellers' Club, The, 71
Trevelyan, Sir Charles, 76
Trinity College, Cambridge, 'feast' at, 108
Trunk Roads, Government Advisory Committee on, 11

Tunisia, 86

Union Club, The, 70
Unité d'Habitation, Marseilles, 84

Vaughan Thomas, Wynford, 105
Venice, 121

Wallace, Charlotte, 32
Ward, Mrs. Humphrey, 76
Waugh, Evelyn, 59
Weaver, Sir Lawrence, 37, 126
Webb, Philip, 114
Welinski, Ruth, 64
Wells, H. G., 127
Welsh Guards, The, 71, 119, 124
Wentworth Woodhouse, 72
Westminster Abbey, Lloyd George memorial in, 48; fragment at Portmeirion, 99
Whistler, Rex, 124
Whitelaw, William, 108
Williamsburg, 58
Williams-Ellis, Amabel, is courted by author, 76; and birthday at Caprira, 78, 87, 102, 105; and Diamond Wedding of, 111, 118, 126; and with the author at Portmeirion, *plate 8*
Williams-Ellis, Sir Clough, ninetieth birthday of, 104–5; Diamond Wedding of, 111; inspecting roof timbers at Dalton Hall, *plate 3a*; with Lady Williams-Ellis at Portmeirion, *plate 8*
Windsor Castle, 106
Wolfe, Edward, 87
Wright, Frank Lloyd, 60
Wyatt, James, 123

Young, Michael, 10–11